PUPPETRY FOR BEGINNERS

PUPPETRY

FOR

BEGINNERS

By

ARTHUR B. ALLEN

WELLS GARDNER, DARTON & CO., LTD.
REDHILL   SURREY

PUPPETRY FOR BEGINNERS
First Published in this Series
1 9 4 7

✱

By
WELLS GARDNER, DARTON & CO., LTD.,
49, Brighton Road, Redhill, Surrey

Printed and Bound in Great Britain by
Love & Malcomson Ltd., Redhill, Surrey

A graded sequence in puppet work, especially designed for use in schools, giving a *sound start* to school or home circle in puppet work. The art of making simple puppets, stage and scenery, of producing simple puppet plays, is thoroughly examined.

CONTENTS

STAGE ONE

STAGE TWO

STAGE THREE

PUPPETRY FOR BEGINNERS

STAGE ONE

CHAPTER ONE

WHY PUPPETRY?

SOME years ago puppetry was considered to be childish. The idea of grown-ups playing with dolls was taken as being the first stage to incarceration in a lunatic asylum.

That phase has passed. It is true that there are people who still think it regrettable that adults should spend their time among these childish things. But then there are still people at liberty who think that women should remain in the home, that men only should have the vote and that a cocktail is a collection of birds' feathers.

These things will be until the end of time. We must accept them, and feel sorry for them, for their ignorance has passed out of the blissful stage and has reached the angle of the idiotic.

We have to deal with people who do not believe as these idiots do. We have to deal with an ever-increasing crowd of folk who see in the Model Theatre all the fun of the fair. We have to deal with the rank and file of a popular movement.

Puppetry has become a popular movement. A national movement. More than that even : puppetry has become an international movement. It will be in the irony of things if, after having castigated all politicians as mere puppets, the puppet theatre achieves that desirable interrelationship of good will which the politicians so singularly have failed to give us. It is well within the realms of possibility, for if tennis balls can precipitate a war, as once they did, then puppets can well bring about a world peace.

Why not ?

What are puppets ?

Puppets are little figures.

Some are flat. Some are round. And some are jointed. Some work with rods. Some are controlled by strings. All are expressive of some human emotion or passion. All are reflective of some philosophy. Even of some antisophy. All reflect some mood, gay, bebonair, unhappy, despondent. The puppet is always positive. One cannot imagine a negative puppet. A puppet has a personality.

I made a puppet once who could act supremely well, when he chose. When the mood was upon him and he did not choose to act supremely well, he developed a slipping pelvis and his actions were more Rabelaisan than Rabelais' own stories !

I called him Gussie.

It seemed to fit. . . .

A puppet has a personality, never question that. If you do so you will find him self-assertive and convincing in spite of yourself.

I began this *Introduction* with the question, *Why puppetry ?* I feel very tempted to ask, *why not ?*

And why not indeed ?

A puppet is a little figure made by hands, imbued with a mischievous personality. Make a puppet and you make a friend. Make several puppets and you possess your own repertory company.

Your own repertory company.

Think of it.

You possess a group of actors and actresses who are—

"The best actors in the world, either for tragedy, comedy, history, pastoral, pastoral-comical, historical-pastoral, tragical-historical, tragical-comical-historical-pastoral, scene individable, or poem unlimited : Seneca cannot be too heavy, nor Plautus too light. For the law of writ and of liberty these are the only men "—to quote our old and verbose friend and stable-philosopher, Polonius.

Your own repertory company.

You can put on your own plays, your favourite plays. You have all had the secret wish to see once again a play you saw long ago. Theatres have a reluctance in the staging of past plays, unless they are long past. So you may not see that play again. If, however, you can get the script you can produce your own version of that play. And you will enjoy doing so even more than you enjoyed the original production.

Why ?

Because it is your *own* production.

The puppet theatre brings the professional theatre right into your own house, right up to your own fireside. It is better than having your home-cinema. In the home-cinema you have nothing to do save plug into the electric point and let the wheels revolve and pray hard that the fuses will not blow out on you !

Your own theatre gives you hours of pleasurable occupation building the theatre, fixing the lighting, painting and designing the scenery and the costumes, cutting, carving, shaping, humanising the puppets, selecting the play, rehearsing the play, and then—then producing the play.

And it is "All me own work, Mum ! All done by hand ! "

Literature, art, music, woodwork, needlework, metal work, electricity, all link hands and make of your work an artistic entity, an individual creation, a piece of yourself.

Why puppetry ?

Why not, indeed.

It is the world of Lilliput with yourself as king.

So, indeed, why not ?

CHAPTER TWO

I HAVE already indicated in " Why Puppetry ? " some of the tangible reasons why you should develop the art of the model theatre within your own home. Let me now go a little deeper and examine how much we we can derive from puppetry.

This is not to be a serious dissertation upon the psychological value of puppetry, although there is a psychological significance to be found therein.

I want here to indicate the sources of interest and of pleasure which are attendant upon the work.

First there is the play. First and last there is the play. The *raison d'être* of puppet work, the be-all and end-all of puppetry, the alpha and omega of puppetry is *the play*. What are your favourite plays ? Make a list of these plays. Sort through the list. Select one play, the presentation of which will be well within your capabilities. Do not take this last sentence too seriously. If you want to produce a play and its production introduces problems with which you have not yet grappled, go for it tooth and nail. Stick to it. Learn as you go along. *Produce that play !*

When I gave you the original warning of keeping within the bounds of your own capabilities I meant, and still mean, to warn you against attempting a too ambitious programme before you have learnt some at least of the technique required of production. It is so easy to fog the issue. Nothing discourages a puppeteer-beginner more than a stage littered with puppets in the negligent poses of lassitude. . . . Strings get into a muddle. Legs and arms assume the grotesque of poses. Tempers fly. Hope evaporates and the theatre is thrown at the cat !

Begin simply. Begin well. Go slowly, but go on. Do not be content with one particular form of puppet presentation because you have made a success of that form. It is gratifying to possess the feeling that this was well done. Jolly well done. It is gratifying to receive the praise of the audience. But do not let that praise turn your head. Go on. Try another form and another and another. Go on going on. Don't give up because people do not like your interpretation of a play. It is *your* interpretation, not theirs. Stick to your own conception of the play against all criticism and all comers. *It is your own, a part of yourself.*

And what has happened during all those fascinating hours when you have been preparing your play ? Well, here is my next point.

Second, you are growing more proficient in hand-skill. Your hand is no longer a bunch of bananas, all thumbs and no fingers. You grow skilled in the construction of the puppet and in its manipulation. A difficult thing to acquire. The acquisition of which skill can come only from experience and practice.

Then you are learning something of costume designing, period costume, colour in costume, harmonious *ensembles*. And while it is of course an asset, pleasurable, delightful to enlist the services of the girl friend to make the costumes for your puppets do not remain for ever dependent upon the needlewoman. Make your own costumes. They may look a little queer at first. They may fit only where they touch, but they will fit better as time goes on. If boys in school can make their own puppet costumes—you can. And boys in school *do* make their own and make them well, too. So eschew dependency and wield your own needle and thread. It's good fun, anyway.

You will be designing your own stage sets and adapting this and that for your stage properties. Here your bump of ingenuity becomes developed and that is a valuable social as well as a theatrical asset.

Besides being a puppeteer I am also an amateur producer on the flesh and blood stage. My friends say that they make notes when they see a production for which I am responsible, discovering as many as they can the household treasures and effects I have conscripted for my scenes! I have had to do so, for amateur work has little money to spend upon the barren pastime of hiring properties.

I have had to " make do."

You will have to " make do."

It is not extravagant expenditure that makes for a successful production. It is the creation of a perfect illusion, using all that is to hand. The illusion and not the balance-sheet is the more important factor in all forms of production.

This goes all the way for model theatre work, too.

Third, you have grown to know quite a lot about the physiognomy of the human race! You become not only a portrait modeller, a sculptor, but also a caricaturist.

Fourth, through your critical examination of plays, your play-readings and your assessments of a play's value, you are learning much about plot construction. The secret of successful dialogue dawns upon you and when you come to write your own puppet plays you will be the better equipped.

I want you to consider the writing of your own puppet plays as an integral part of puppet work. Does that sound too difficult a task ? It is not. Shut yourself up in your own library, your own study, your bedroom, the toolshed, the coal cellar even, and write your play *by speaking the dialogue aloud as you do so.* Cut out all the frilly bits. Keep to stark language. Tell the story as a straight story. Tell it as you would tell a story— through conversation. This is your first effort. When you have perfected this form try other forms, the fantastic, the poetic, the introspective, the symbolic, but try straight stuff first. Take a simple fairy story and dramatise that. Make the characters tell their own story in their own way, but make them *speak.* You have to speak when the performance is being presented. You and your friends will be the voices behind the scenes. Your voice and their voices will have to express anger, hate, love, happiness, despair, jubilation, teachery. You and they will have to run through the whole gamut of the emotions, to prepare yourself by writing your own plays, by speaking each part aloud as you write and record the words spoken. That *play* must reach the audience. It *must* convince the audience. It *must* play upon the emotions of the audience. See to it that it does.

Fifth, you gain in organisational experience. You are actor, producer, electrician, designer, stage-manager all in one. A thousand things to think of and only one pair of hands ! Yet you can do it. We all can do it. Establish a system of control and stick to that system. It pays to be methodical in puppet work.

Lastly, you have the whole world of literature, drama, music and art to draw from for your material. You read more. You read widely, deeply. The puppet theatre opens a new vista for you. A new landscape rolls away and away before you. It is yours. All yours. What you began as a pastime has become a hobby and from a hobby has become a culture. A diamond of many facets and all glistening. It is a world you have created for yourself. It is *your* world. That is the significence of puppetry.

It gives you to a new world and gives a new world to you.

CHAPTER THREE

LET us get quite clearly in our mind what we mean when we speak of glove puppets. I think it safe to assume that everyone has watched a performance of Punch and Judy. Then everyone has seen a performance by glove puppets. Punch is a glove puppet. So is Judy. So, too, are all the characters in the play except, of course. Dog Toby, for most showmen have a real live Dog Toby. Some, however, prefer a puppet dog and in this preference I approve. I cannot look at a real live Dog Toby without feeling sorry for the pathetic, wistful animal sitting up there, very bored with it all and not being able just to be a dog. If ever I am arrested by the police I have a feeling it will be for kidnapping a real life Dog Toby. So let this stand on record as a prophecy :

Now—how can we make a glove puppet ? Well, here is one method :

1. Get a cardboard tube of sufficient width in diameter to allow the free insertion of a finger. Cut off about three inches from the tube. This forms the basis of the head. (*Fig.* IA.)

2. Around this tube model the head, leaving about half an inch protruding at the base to form the neck. (*Fig* IB.)

3. Pack the head well. Make it well rounded. There is always a tendency when using a tube to over-elongate a head. This may suit a character part. It

would suit the part of Scrooge admirably, but would be useless in so jovial a face as Mr. Pickwick. So—well round the head. (*Fig.* 1C.)

4. For your modelling material you may use either newspaper pulp and an adhesive, or Barbola, or a

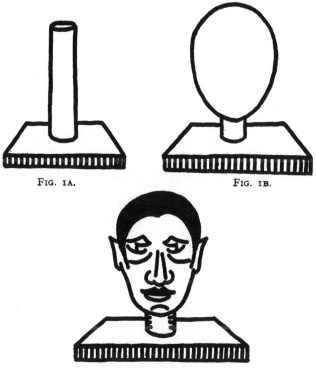

FIG. 1A.   FIG. 1B.

FIG. 1C.

mixture of size and sawdust. This latter medium is terrible messy, so my advice to you is to leave it alone. Yet with sawdust one can produce a finish very much akin to plastic wood.

5. When the head is modelled stand it to dry. Watch that it does not roll over when drying. A good

plan to prevent this roll is to drive a long nail into a piece of flat wood and stand the head over the nail, so that it remains in an upright position, and so dries evenly and well.

6. To make the hands use flexible wire. If you can get a wire which is covered with cotton so well and good. If not it does not matter. Bend the wire into a hand shape and twist the ends into the wrist. (*Fig.* 2A.)

7. Using pink wool and a bodkin, bind the wool round and round the wire, working all round the shape. As you bind the wool you will begin to fill in the space between the wires. As you near the middle, stop the

FIG. 2A.   FIG. 2B.

binding and begin to thread the woollen strands over and under until the palm of the hand is net-worked in wool. (*Fig.* 2B.)

The hand is now ready for fixing to the body.

8. The " body " is a cloth sheath. A glove.

The " body " stretches from the neck to the enveloping base into which the hand is thrust. (*Fig.* 2C.)

9. Two arms, with shaped hands, form part of the body.

10. No feet are necessary in the ordinary glove puppet. If you do add feet you must remember that these feet are dummies.

FIG. 2C.

Now turn to my illustrations and you will see clearly indicated the various stages of the glove puppet.

The hands of a glove puppet can, of course, be carved out of wood. If you look at my illustration (*Fig.* 3) you will see how this can be done.

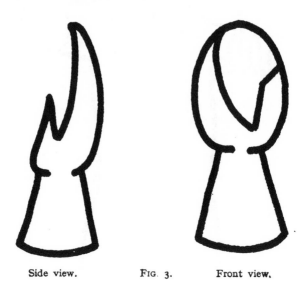

Side view.   FIG. 3.   Front view.

CHAPTER FOUR

THERE are stringed puppets or marionettes which spring into action by overhead manipulation. There are glove puppets which are operated from beneath the stage. There are rod puppets which are operated from above the stage, from below the stage and from the stage level.

But since I shall be dealing with these various types elsewhere I want to write of the round puppet figure operated from above the stage at this juncture.

You will notice I say *round* puppet figure—a puppet figure " in the round." There are puppet figures " in the round " and there are puppet figures " in the flat."

Here we speak of the three-dimensional puppet figure operated from above.

One of the most successful rod figure plays I ever saw was a version of *Jack and the Beanstalk,* performed by a class of children in a poor school in the East End of London.

I made notes of their work and here are my notes:

1. Twist one end of a piece of flexible wire into an oval. This is for the head. So you have an oval wire loop at the end of a piece of wire. The long end becomes the backbone, and from the crown of the head (the oval) to the bottom of the wire should be about four inches in length. At the end farthest from the oval turn the wire about a pencil and make a small loop. Through this loop the legs will join the body. (*Fig.* 4A.)

2. Take a second and shorter piece of wire. Twist around the backbone at the shoulder level. Twist two small loops, one at each end of this right-angled wire. Here the arms will be joined. (*Fig.* 4B.)

3. To make the body use long strips of newspaper covered on one side with an adhesive. Cut these strips

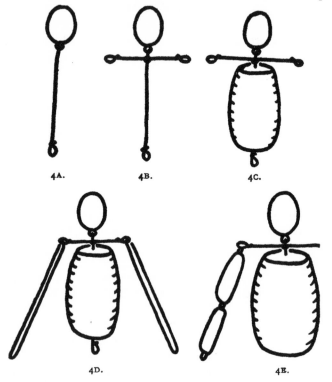

4A.   4B.   4C.

4D.   4E.

half an inch short of the depth of the body, thus leaving a quarter of an inch for the shoulders and a quarter of an inch for the hips. (*Fig.* 4C.)

Wind the newspaper strips until you have a sufficient thickness for the trunk.

4. Take pieces of twine or fairly thick string. Pass one piece of string through the wire loop at the left shoulder. Adjust the length of the string when *doubled* to run from shoulder to *wrist*.

Repeat for right shoulder and so lay the foundation for the right arm. (*Fig.* 4D.)

5. Cut long triangular strips of newspaper. Beginning at the widest end of the strip, stick this tapering length of newspaper to the upper arm. Wind round and round and so make the arm shape.

6. Repeat No. 5 for the lower arm.

7. Repeat Nos. 5 and 6 so that both arms are made in a like manner. See that the lengths of the paper are coincident or you will get one arm fatter than the other. Remember also for elbow to wrist does not need to be as stout as from shoulder to elbow. (*Fig.* 5E.)

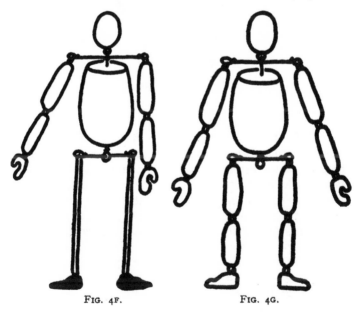

FIG. 4F.   FIG. 4G.

Leave the string exposed at the elbow.

8. To make the legs, begin on the thighs first. Use the tapering newspaper strips once again. Pad the thighs well. (*Figs.* 4F and 4G.)

9. Remember that the shins must not be as substantial as the thighs. Even Falstaff's shins although well covered were not as stout as his elephantine thighs.

FIG. 5.

10. To make the hands use flexible wire. Twist one end around the twine wrist, still exposed after the padding of the arms. Bend the wire into the shape of a boxing glove. Oversew the frame with wool, using a bodkin. You can use thin white string instead of wool if you prefer. Then, as the oversewing thickens towards the palm, sew under and over until the whole boxing glove shape is covered with string. Here are the hands made and fastened to the wrist. (*Fig.* 5.)

We have now an oval-headed figure (the oval still showing in bare wire) complete with trunk, arms and legs and hands. The exposed twine at the elbows and knee allows for movement.

11. Cut the feet out of odd pieces of wood and sole with thin sheet lead. You fix the feet to the ankles by a screw-eye driven into the wood. Open the eye of the

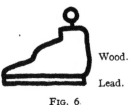

Wood.

Lead.

FIG. 6.

screw with a pair of pliers, slip the string loop inside the screw and close up. (*Fig.* 6.)

12. To the oval still waiting to receive the head, fasten a piece of stout wire for the crown. Twist this wire around the head wire at the crow point. See that this wire is of sufficient length to go well up into the "flies," i.e., the upper reaches of the theatre. This is the operating wire— the operating rod. (*Fig.* 7.)

13. To make the head, screw up a ball of paper so that it is oval in shape and just fits inside the wire oval. It will help if you wet the paper first, but do not pulp the paper.

FIG. 7.

14. With pieces of tissue paper, Gloy, or flour paste or another form of adhesive, pad all round the head until the oval wire is covered.

15. Now with flat pieces of tissue stick the whole surface over until you have a smooth covering to the head.

16. Out of sticky tissue paper, pulped in the adhesive, model the nose and the ears and the forehead.

The basic structure of the head is now finished and out of its crown rises the wire rod.

When you have dressed your puppet, painted its face, added the hair and the costume, you are ready to begin.

At the end of the guide wire bend a triangular shape to give you a finger hold.

You operate the puppet from above the stage, making the figure waddle through its actions by half-turns of the vertical wire.

An examination of my illustrations will show you in greater detail how all this may be done.

This is a simple form of puppet. It is popular among school children and among beginners because it is so very easy to manipulate. Anyone can make a rod puppet work.

Some puppeteers like to make the arms and hands of the rod puppets move more realistically, for even sticks among us do not go through life all the time with our arms dangling by our sides!

So—string the hands as I suggest in my illustrations and so add another movement to the figure.

This movement of the arms upon a rod puppet has this technical advantage: it acquaints the newcomer to puppet work with some elementary lessons in puppet control.

CHAPTER FIVE

VARIOUS FORMS OF CUT-OUTS

CHILDREN often introduce themselves or are introduced to model theatre work through cut-out figures.

In the old days, when cigarette cards were interesting and contained pictures other than machines of destruction or portraits of film stars, it was possible to get *Characters from Dickens* and *Characters from Thackeray*. These we cut out when we were boys and strung upon an endless thread belt, grouping the characters from any one given story together (*Fig.* 8). Such an invention made out of a box, some thread and some cigarette cards gives a very limited scope in terms of action, but it gave us tremendous fun. At least the figures *moved* and so were an improvement upon the flat drawing, however interesting that drawing might have been.

Let us now examine this idea of cut-out figures, for we approach a fertile field. Nor need adults turn up their noble noses in scorn at so elementary a beginning. A passing acquaintance with model theatre work will introduce the newcomers to the " penny plain and tuppenny coloured " theatres which were all the vogue those years ago. And if my reader has not yet seen a performance of *The Miller and His Men*, then, by the Lord Harry, he has not entered this romantic world.

Although a child may derive much pleasure from cutting out little figures upon a cigarette card and working them with an endless belt of thread, this is almost entirely a child's activity. Not to be scorned because of that, but I suggest the adult will try at once

Fig. 8.

Continuous band of string braced around a match or short pencil.
The figures cut out. The scenery painted on back of box.

Fig. 9.

for a more mobile form of dramatic expression. So I propose to leave this earlier form, saying no more of it than my illustration shows. What is the next stage, therefore ?

Let us get the essentials stated first of all.

A cut-out is a figure designed in the flat—a flat figure in cardboard, thick paper, even in wood. It represents a character in the story or in the play. It is introduced on to the stage by means of a rod or thin " stave " or wire, attached to one side of the base. The figure therefore is cut out in the flat, firmly mounted upon a small base and attached at one end of the base to the rod. (*Fig.* 9.)

The base must be of sufficient weight to maintain the figure in an upright position. The base must also be as small as is possible in terms of balance and ballast. It must not obtrude too heavily upon the eye of the audience. The rod must be as slender as is consistent with its work and that, too, must be as unobtrusive as possible.

So the cut-out figure has three parts :

(*a*) The figure itself.

(*b*) The base.

(*c*) The manipulating rod.

Let us suppose we wish to stage a little show at Christmas-time. We want perhaps to show the Carol Singers, standing outside the Manor House. We begin to turn up the Christmas Numbers of the national periodicals until we find a group, *as a drawing*, which will serve. The main sources of wealth for such groups will be found in such publications as *The Sphere, The Tatler, The Illustrated London News, Holly Leaves, Good Housekeeping* and *The Saturday Evening Post* (American, but obtainable at any good bookstall).

We cut out the picture of carol singers, cut out the entire picture first and mount upon thin white cardboard. Press flat and leave to dry, keeping the picture *under pressure* while drying. This obviates the intensely annoying habit art paper possesses of cockling or bending into a slight arc. It is absolutely essential for the picture to come out flat after drying. (*Fig.* 10.)

When thoroughly dry, take a sharp pair of scissors, small scissors preferably, and cut out the group of waits.

FIG. 10.

The carol singers will light their scores with lanterns. Some of these lanterns they will hold aloft by hand. Others they may hold aloft in the traditional manner, upon a form of shepherd's crook. You will want the scene lighted. Realistically the light will come from :

(*a*) The windows of the manor house.

(*b*) The lanterns.

(*c*) The moon, if so be there is a moon. In this, our own scene of the carol singers, there jolly well is going to be a moon !

Take a piece of stout wire. Bend crookshape to hold the lantern. Out of cardboard and yellow cellophane make a tiny lantern just big enough to take the smallest electric bulb procurable. Put the electric light inside the lantern, bring the flex down the stave to behind the figure of the lantern-bearer. Carry the flex along the rod *on the side farthest from the audience* and out into the wings of the little theatre. Here you fix it to a tiny switchboard complete with battery.

The group itself you will fix into a base. For a group of this nature I prefer using the grooved wooden base obtainable from *Hobbies*. The rod may be either a strip of galvanised wire, pulled taut before cutting, to remove all " kinks " and curves, or you may use thin pieces of strip wood about three-sixteenths of an inch thick. This will be strong enough for the purpose.

Paint the background, the manor house, upon cardboard. Mount the cardboard upon a bracer frame first to prevent twisting and bending. Where you want the lighted windows to show, cut these windows out of the cardboard, use cardboard strips to show the latticework or the leaden panes. Behind the network of leads stick a deep red cellophane sheet, or ordinary greaseproof paper washed with a crimson Mandarin ink (a form of Indian ink).

Cut out the moon. Make a circular moon. It looks better and brighter and leaves no doubt in the minds of the audience. . . . Stick orange or a pale yellow cellophane sheet behind this. Or again, colour ordinary greaseproof paper with orange or pale yellow Mandarin ink and use that. Maybe you would like to show some stars, too. Here you will have a little difficulty for stars are small. Very small to cut out of cardboard. Use here either a decorative leather punch and knock out the star shape or pierce out the star shape, using a cobbler's awl, which is sharp and slender and can be worked upon a very small space.

Back the stars with a light blue, a cold blue, cellophane sheet. A small flashlamp bulb behind the back scene will give you all the light you need.

For snow, use cottontwool. If stuck upon the overhanging eaves of the house it gives a most realistic effect.

FIG. 11.
Design for backcloth. The Manor House.

The stage is ready. The curtain goes back. The scene is exposed. A writer's essay on Christmas Eve and all in the English tradition. The characters arrive in the half-light. The electrically lighted lantern held aloft is not yet burning. The characters arrive in the half-light, therefore. They take up their position. The light goes up. They are seen now. The carol begins. It may be a gramophone record. It may be a choir of voices behind the stage. It does not matter which. The scene creates the Christmas atmosphere and there you are.

You have presented a cut-out scene based partly upon a printed design and partly upon your own creative work. (*Fig.* 11.)

The next step is to do your own designing throughout. Once again let us suppose you wish to present a Christmas story. This time, however, in several parts. Let us take this stage by stage.

Scene One.—On the Road to Bethlehem. Here come all manner of folk of high and low degree. The narrator, the voice behind the stage who tells the story, tells of how *The degree went forth from Cæsar Augustus that all the world should be taxed.* Here come the folk back to their native hearths—to be counted.

The procession passes. At the end come Joseph and Mary. Joseph leads the ass whereon Mary rides.

Scene Two.—The Inn Door. Joseph and Mary enter the inn yard. The innkeeper appears through the door. There is no room. The innkeeper returns inside. Joseph and Mary move on.

Scene Three.—The Stable. Joseph and Mary by the side of the crib. Animals in the background. The shepherds enter, speak, retire. The Three Wise Men enter, speak, retire.

Joseph and Mary and The Child are left alone. " Hark, the Herald Angels sing," comes softly over the scene. (*Curtain.*)

These figures and groups of figures can be designed by yourself. Draw them upon thick cartridge paper, cut out and mount upon cardboard. Colour.

It is wiser to use opaque colours for model theatre work. Colours in the style of poster, showcard or New Art Powder Colours. These give blazing surfaces of flat colour. If you want to tone down the colours, if you feel that their brilliancy strikes the wrong note in the setting, then mix black, or white or grey, with them. If you mix black you will make the *shades*, the very dark colours.

If you mix white you will get the *tints*, the pastel effects. If you mix grey you will make what are known as the *shaded tints*, soft colours which lie midway between the shades and the tints.

A little knowledge of colour and colour theory is necessary to successful model theatre work. I strongly advise you to use the Ostwald System of Colour Harmony with its eight standard hues: yellow, orange, red, purple, blue, turquoise, sea-green and leafgreen, black (*n*), white (*a*), and grey (*g*).

The (*n*), (*a*) and (*g*) indices are necessary when ordering, for these are the values which produce the best results. Do not therefore ask for black, ask for Ostwald Black (*n*) and you will get what you want.

Stick to opaque colours. Water-colours are too delicate. They can be used to advantage in tinting, for example, a stained-glass window, because they work up softer than even Mandarin inks. But for all surface decoration, scenery and costume, paint in opaque colours.

If it is your intention to give many performances of your show then you may find the cardboard unsuitable. Even with careful handling cardboard is easily damaged. So use then three-ply wood. Cut with a fine saw, sand-paper the edges before colouring and then colour in opaque colours. There is no need to size the wood first for these heavy colours contain a certain percentage of gum and the paint goes into the grain of the wood, slight as the grain may be. The final result is a flat, matt, colourful surface.

Wooden cut-outs should be mounted in wooden bases.

We now come to a development arising out of the cut-out figure. Perhaps it would be wiser to say arising *because* of the cut-out figure. This is the *shadow show*. (*Fig.* 12.)

The figures for your first shadow show may be of a similar type as for the ordinary cut-out show. With this exception, you need not colour the figures. But if I were you I should colour the figures, for then you can use them *either* for an ordinary open show *or* a shadow play. The colour does not appear, of course, in the straightforward shadow show.

Shadow shows may be of varying forms. Indeed, they are a study and a technique in themselves. But for our purpose I shall deal with the three elementary kinds.

Fit your theatre front with either a sheet of opalescent glass or with a frame upon which greaseproof paper has

FIG. 12.

been evenly stretched. You must see to it that no light escapes through the side or you will distract the attention of the audience. It is an amazing but nevertheless a true fact, that a chink of light will divert the attention of the audience and perhaps spoil a well-designed, well-constructed stage presentation. Human nature being what it is, curiosity is aroused. People want to know what is going on behind that chink, rather than watch what is going on upon the open stage !

For the light source use either one gas-filled high-powered white electric bulb, or several smaller ones mounted upon a base. Fix each lamp to a sliding beam so that you can arrange the lighting in a varying degree of intensity if you wish. Or you can use tubular lighting. Whichever you use make it possible to concentrate the light hard upon the back of your screen.

Test this intensity with a figure. You must obtain a clearly defined shadow upon the screen. Clean edges, not woolly edges. Pitch up the light until you get as black a shadow as you can manage.

In the old days we used to employ a row of short, well-protected candles. To-day with electricity we can dispense with candles. Even so, candles make fine shadows.

The first of your shadow shows may utilise your ordinary cut-out figures, made of either cardboard or wood.

The story unfolds in the usual manner. The audience sees the shadows passing instead of the coloured figures.

FIG. 13.

A—Body. B—Working arm and hand holding stick and bundle. CC—Working legs. Fasten each foot to separate rods and work alternative strokes.

The second attempt at a shadow show may find you wishing to introduce certain *actions*. Movement of feet and hands and head. The movement can be achieved by constructing special figures. See my illustrations. (*Fig.* 13.)

Or you may not wish for movement but you may want colour. To introduce colour into a shadow show you must work in " transparencies."

Draw out your figure first, in pencil. Then outline the figure, using a wide ball-nose pen. A Redis pen gives the best result here. When the ink is dry cut out all the cardboard *inside* the heavy ink lines. You possess now a skeleton outline of your figure, somewhat after the style of the leads in a stained-glass window. Using coloured greaseproof paper or cellophane sheets, back up in the colours you require. (*Fig.* 14.)

This figure when placed between the light and the screen will throw upon the screen a dense black outline filled in with colour. I would advise you to keep to motionless figures for colour cut-outs. To make transparencies in this style of figure gives you too many problems at first. You can graduate into motion figures later if you so wish.

Some puppeteers affect a contemptuous attitude towards the cut-out. This is as absurd as it is a clear indication of their own ignorance. One can

FIG. 14.

present crowd scenes and many another scene too complicated for string puppets and certainly impossible for glove puppets.

Cut-out figures have their place in model theatre work even if only because they make pageantry possible.

CHAPTER SIX

A PUPPET FIGURE IN A PLASTIC MATERIAL

BEFORE one begins to carve the marionette proper I think it is a good experience to make a little jointed figure out of a plastic material. The drawback to creating figures in a plastic medium lies in the weight of the finished model. As I point out elsewhere, weight may be, indeed, can be, a useful adjunct to a puppet, but too much weight brings trouble to the manipulator.

But from experience I have found that newcomers to puppetry gain confidence more quickly if they make plastic figures first.

Confidence is one of the rudimentary essentials in puppet work. With confidence a new-born puppeteer can work wonders; without it, nothing will come except chaos. There is no room for chaos in a model theatre, you may take my word for it !

Plastic medium figures have weight. Dead weight when compared with the carved figures of the experienced puppeteer. It is necessary therefore to have the figures on the small side. I have the characters of *Twelfth Night* all created in Barbola. These are little figures barely three inches high. So it can be done.

I include such a form in this work for there is a large section of the community who can work better in miniature than on a larger scale.

To make this diminutive figure I would ask you to read the following notes in conjunction with my illustration. (*Fig.* 15.)

1. Roll a circular head and pinch a stump for the

neck. Using a nail file or some such similar instrument,
fashion the features. Model only the main planes of
the face, the forehead, the eyebrows, the nose, cheekbones and chin.

2. The trunk to be in one piece. Notice the slight
flattening where the arms will join the body.

3. The legs and thighs, the arms and hands, and feet,
make from rolls of Barbola.

FIG. 15.

4. While the Barbola is still in a modelling state
insert the screw-eyes.   Use the smallest screw-eyes
possible and *twist* these into the preparation rather than
thrust them in.   The thread of the screw will then hold
firmly.   If a screw works loose and tends to come out
dip the screw into seccotine and reinsert.   Once the figure
is clothed the screws will hold without further trouble.

A play by such a figure or by such figures may be
performed upon the dining-room table.

Plastic wood may be substituted for Barbola, but this
is more expensive.   Otherwise the substitution is perfectly
suitable.

CHAPTER SEVEN

IT is not always possible to have at hand materials and tools for carving and creating a wooden figure. Sometimes you are caught napping. You have lent your tools—not a very wise procedure, but common enough among puppeteers. You want to make a puppet and the night is cold and the tools are in the shed at the bottom of the garden and you are by the fireside and in your slippers. You still want to make a puppet. How will you do this without apparatus ? Well, there is a way, and here it is.

I do not claim that this method makes a perfect puppet, but I have seen some excellent puppets made by this method. Also it is a form of puppet-making that can be done by those who cannot use tools ; invalids and children in a hospital, for example. It is amazing how much puppetry *is* done in hospitals, in children's wards and among invalids who have an earnest desire to preserve social contacts.

Puppetry is an accomplishment. Do you recall how in the last century it was vital for social progress for an individual, particularly a girl, to possess some "accomplishments " ? If you could sing or play a musical instrument or recite you were invited everywhere, unless, that is, your " accomplishment " was so unbelievably bad that even the nineteenth-century drawing-room could not tolerate it. Which presupposes a state of society which could not exist.

Puppetry enables you to " do a turn " at a home concert. There are so many people who simply cannot because they dare not recite or sing or otherwise perform in public. But give these same people a little theatre, some figures and a play and all their nervousness disappears and they become successful puppet masters.

Let us not lose sight of the social side of puppetry in our search for technique. The social side is an important part of puppetry.

Now what can we do ?

All our material is unavailable at the moment. Yet we shall make our puppet.

1. Get a ball of thick string. If you live in the country binder-twine is marvellous stuff for this work. Thick string or binder-twine then.

2. You will want either five small curtain rings or some flexible wire. I prefer the wire, but invalids or young children will find the rings easier to work.

3. If you use the wire, then bend it into an oval shape, twist the ends of the wire for the neck and overlap the free ends after twisting, thus making a loop. This makes the head and neck.

4. Now twist a piece of wire into the shape of a boxing glove. Twist the free ends to make the wrist and then loop. Make two of these shapes, of course.

5. Now twist the foot shape, shape the ankle and leave a loop. Two of these.

If you use small curtain rings bend one into an oval for the head, two more ovals for the hands, and two more for the feet. Use a larger ring for the head than for either hands or feet.

We have now five metal loops and a ball of twine, thick twine.

6. Tie the head loop on to one end of the twine. Do this either by using a knot or by looping the twine through the ring, bending the shorter end over and then

binding the two pieces together just *under* the ring. To bind the ends use thread wound round and round.

From the tied neck measure eight inches of twine, at the end farthest from the neck make a loop-binding the ends with thread. Make this loop of just sufficient opening that the twine itself will pass through easily. Allow only a minimum of play within the loop.

7. Now take sixteen inches of twine, pass this length through the new loop (as given in No. 6 above) until the half-way mark is reached. That will give you eight inches each side of the loop. This hempen inverted " U " will ultimately form the legs.

8. At the two free ends of the leg strings bind a metal loop. These will be the feet.

So now we have the head loop fastened to the trunk string. A loop at the waist line of the trunk string through which passes the leg strings. At the end of each leg string we have the feet loops.

We have still to fix the hands and arms.

9. Take a piece of twine which *when doubled* reaches from the neck to midway between waist and feet. Find the mid-point in this string and at this point bind this arm string to the trunk string just below the neck wire.

10. At either end of the arm strings bind the hand loops.

Our *skeleton* is complete.

We have to give it a three-dimensional figure. Proceed now as follows :

(*a*) Pulp newspaper and with the pulp model the head about the wire loop. Press firmly so that no air pockets are left between each additional amount of pulp used to build up the head. If after you have pulped your newspaper in water you take it out of the pan, squeeze out all the surplus water and then pound the pulp into a thin solution of flour paste or gum arabic, you will find the pulp models in a much more satisfactory style.

Smooth the surface of the face as you go along. Add nose and ears and eyebrows.

(b) Using paper pulp and an adhesive, model the hands and feet. If you notch a piece of lead piping or a small piece of sheet lead and pinch this lead into the feet wire you can then model around wire and lead and not only

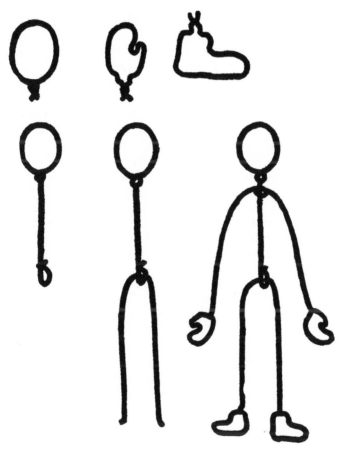

FIG. 16.

fashion the feet but give yourself the necessary weight as you go along.

(c) Arms and legs must each be in two parts. The upper and lower arm. The thighs and the shins. Leave the raw twine showing at the shoulders and at the elbows, at the hips and at the knees and the ankles. This makes for flexibility.

(d) To pad out the arms take strips of newspaper and cut into long triangular lengths, like elongated tapering pennants. Gum these strips well before using, then, when gummed, fold the broad end round the string which is to be the skeleton of the upper arm and wind round and round. As you get nearer and nearer to the pointed end the middle of the upper arm begins to rise. The final effect is of a long bead threaded upon the string. (See *Fig.* 4.)

By this method build up the arms and the legs. The trunk of the puppet is still an emaciated piece of twine !

(e) Using the newspaper pulp and the adhesive, once again build the body around the backbone. Shape the shoulders, taper in to the waist. You leave the trunk until last so that you can regulate the size in accordance with the space required for a perfect freedom for the arms.

Your puppet is now ready for dressing. Now look at my illustration and you will see how this puppet built from waste stuff grows up under your hand.

CHAPTER EIGHT

SCENERY and design in the theatre allow the artist to join the team of puppeteers. It is his work to fashion the costumes and to design the stage sets. In puppetry you may find yourself not only making your own puppets, but also being your own electrician, writing your own plays and designing your own scenes. This is valuable experience, especially if you will remember that at first you cannot possibly be an expert in all branches. You will learn. You will acquire knowledge, practical knowledge, and you will find tremendous pleasure in this new world of applied art and craft and literature.

The designing of scenery may lead you astray. You must remember that in the presentation of a play, it is the play that is the most important part of the production. Your skill in the making of the puppets, your adroit manipulation of the puppets, your beautifully designed costumes and stage sets, are no more and no less than the methods and modes employed to guarantee that the audience cannot fail to appreciate the play.

If you keep in mind the correct sequence of play production, whether by human actors or by puppets, you will not lose sight of this importance of the play.

As you read play after play, you will be seeking a play, *the* play which you feel you simply *must* produce. Why do you want to produce that play? It may be because you like the story. It may be because you feel instinctively that the philosophy of the play can only be revealed

39

by a certain type of production, and that type of production is definitely your type. You feel you have discovered a play which you really can interpret.

You see ? It is the *play* you wish to interpret. You have not chosen a play because it gives you an excellent excuse to " show off " your marvellous efficiency with this or that type of puppet. You have not chosen the play because it will reveal your skill as a puppeteer— only reveal your skill as a puppeteer.

If you do wish to show off, and only to " show off," then do not insult the writer of the play, whoever he may be, by using his play for your own exhibitionism. Be honest. Choose a play because you want to perform *that* play and no other. Once you have chosen that play, let yourself go. Put into the production every ounce of skill you possess, and get the story " across the footlights " to the audience.

And that brings us once again to stage design.

In puppetry, as in the theatre, you will find it very tempting to make of your scene a beautiful picture to the exclusion of all else. I once saw a production of *Macbeth* in which the scenes were so beautifully designed that I, for one, gazed in admiration at the art before me, and completely forgot the play itself.

That is bad production. The producer had produced a play that the audience might hear the words and see the actions. But he had allowed the stage designer to overshadow his own production until the picture killed the action.

Keep clear of that mistake.

Your scenery must be so designed as to enhance the beauty of the play, or stress the spirit of the play without destroying the play.

Let me give you two examples. I once saw a puppet play production of *Aladdin*. It was a really fine piece of work until we came to the scene in the treasure cave.

Then the trouble began. The designer had been hypnotised by the idea of a cave filled with gems and sparkling diamonds. He had sprinkled every square inch of that interior with pieces of glass, sequins and other devices that caught the light and twinkled. Twinkled ! That scene *danced* with multitudinous points of light until every eye was held and every mind distracted away from the play. We did not care about the quarrel between Aladdin and the Magician any more. All we were conscious of was those twinkling, dancing, scintillating points of coloured lights.

This was bad production. It subordinated the story to mere cleverness in creating an illusion. The power of the story was destroyed at that point.

Then I saw another production where the story was set in the slums. There was little upon that stage except a painted wall and a scene through a window. It was a stark, terrible picture of conditions in the slums. It created the right atmosphere. It put all of us into the right mind to receive the message of the play. We *understood* that play because we had been helped in our understanding by the design of the set.

So when you begin to design your scenery, put right out of your head all idea of showing the audience how clever you are as an artist. Aim to show your deep understanding as an *interpreter*. The pictures you create in your scenes must help create an atmosphere in which this particular set of characters will live and talk, and act quite naturally.

If you are really keen upon stage designing, you will benefit greatly by reading up the history of stage design. It is an interesting history. I cannot in this short work give you even a skeleton outline of its evolution, but there are one or two points I would like you to remember.

When plays were performed in church in the Middle Ages they were surrounded by all the severe beauty of

church architecture. The characters wore bright costumes, since the plays were taken from the Bible and so
were Eastern in spirit, and these bright costumes showed
up splendidly in the half-light of the church.

In Elizabethan times, when the playhouses were
extremely popular and strolling players could be seen
visiting most of the big towns, the players had no need
to transport great loads of scenery from place to place.
All they had to do was to find a stage. There they
played their play, without scenery, whether it was in a
baronial hall or in a courtyard of an inn, open to the sky
above, surrounded by a gallery where the quality sat
or stood. We have still such a place, the "New Inn," in
Gloucester. The players did not bother their heads over
scenery. If the scene was in a wood, they put up a large
notice which might read *In the Forest of Arden*, or another
for the next scene, *A Room—The Palace.* So they went
on, telling the audience where the action was supposed
to be taking place and they left it to the imagination of
the audience to create the scene for themselves. They
could do this, for it seems that the audiences of those
days had more imagination than the audiences of to-day
possess !

If money was to be spent upon a company's equipment,
that money went into the purchasing of costumes. The
early companies sometimes possessed rich wardrobes.
They spent no money upon scenery as we know it and
even if they had they could not have used that scenery.
There was nowhere to erect it.

The Elizabethans went to see the play and to hear the
players. The play was the entertainment, not the
spectacle, not the picture upon the stage.

During the Restoration Period the theatres were built
to a different style. To begin with, the old idea of the
open-air theatre, that is a theatre with the pit open to
the sky, was discarded. The new theatres were roofed

over. The addition of a cover-all roof meant that daylight was very largely excluded and so the actors had to rely upon artificial light. The old theatres following the main plan of the inn yard were square in shape and the audience formed, as it were, part of the play itself, for they surrounded the stage on three sides. The new theatres rejected the square plan and grew rectangular in shape. The stage was shut off from the audience by the proscenium arch, a large picture frame surrounding the front of the stage. But all links with tradition were not lost. The architects of the new theatre introduced *the apron stage*, a semicircular projection which reached out into the audience. The audience sat in front of the stage, not around it, and even with the jutting out of the apron stage only a small part of the audience were in close contact with the players.

The introduction of the closed-in stage with its proscenium arch allowed for the introduction of scenic effects. The stage designer came into his own. The written placards telling the place and scene of the action were required no more.

Inigo Jones was responsible in the main, perhaps, for the introduction of scenic effects. Inigo Jones and Ben Jonson, working together upon the Court Masques, introduced elaborate sets. Jones' pupil was John Webb, who worked with D'Avenant, and D'Avenant is believed to be the one man responsible for popularising the use of scenery in the theatres attended by the public.

From then onwards scenery was accepted as the right and proper adjunct to play productions. But every age did not possess its Inigo Jones and its John Webb.

Slowly stage decoration sank lower and lower until it became a thing of horror to the artist. Form, colour, composition, lighting, these were ignored. Trees were painted as stolid wooden things, standing in rows like toy soldiers. The leaves of the trees hung down like so much washing upon a line. All was dull, uninteresting, without illusion. All was so obviously painted, and painted not by an artist of feeling, but by a hack.

Not only was this neglect of the scene wrong in that it was so obvious to the audience, it was unfair to the actor. Here was the actor, striving with all his power to create an illusion, to take the audience into "a strange new world," and behind him and around him stood, stark and forbidding, the awful scenery which destroyed every movement he made, every idea he tried to re-create.

Something *had* to be done. It was not done until the present century. It began in Germany, where the producers enlisted the services of the artists and designers. They gave definite instructions to those artists and designers. They said to them : " Here is the play we shall produce. Take it. Read it. Study it. Design for it. Make the world upon that stage the identical world in which the play is performed." The artists responded, as they always do respond to responsibility and creative direction.

Stage design was born anew.

The artists realised the need to awaken in the audience the reactions proper to the play. The artists set out to convince the audience that the world created by the dramatist was a real world, not a make-believe world. It was a world of reality with the crudity and squalor of the slums or " the imaginative quality of a poet's dream."

Briefly, and very briefly, these are the major signposts in the history of scenery and design in the theatre. Such a history should help you to keep in mind the essential lessons of *first things first.*

In puppetry you are confronted with no problem of vast expenditure. What you cannot do with pieces of cardboard, three-ply wood, paint, wire, paper and. odd scraps, you need not even attempt to do.

Your stage equipment for scenery need consist of no more than :

1. Thick cardboard. Thin cardboard.
2. Thick paper. A good cartridge paper.
3. Strips of wood for supports and battens.
4. Opaque colours. Use showcard colours.
5. Greaseproof paper for window transparencies, to be coloured with Mandarin-coloured inks.
6. Cellophane sheets for use in No. 5 (above) in place of coloured greaseproof paper and for coloured lights.
7. A fretsaw, a tenon-saw, a sharp knife.
8. A set of good sable brushes. Sables are a little more expensive but they last longer than any other brush. I advise you to get Scholastic Sables, Series 34, in sizes 4, 5 and 6. These may be used for water-colour, showcard colour or coloured inks.

I shall deal with the more practical aspects of scenery design in the following works under the chapter heading of *Scenery*. I shall also deal with specific designs as and when they occur in the development of the work.

CHAPTER NINE

A BRIEF HISTORY OF PUPPETRY

THE beginnings of puppetry are "wropt in mystery." Like Topsy, they seem to have " jest growd." Even the origin of the name is shrouded within the same impenetrable mist.

To-day some people speak of *Marionettes* and some of *Puppets*. The terms are becoming interchangeable. Yet the dictionary when called to our aid gives little help in the matter.

The *King's English Dictionary* gives :

Marionette, n. (F.) a puppet moved by strings.

Puppetry, n. ostentation, affectation.

Puppet, n. (O.F. *paupette*, fr. L. *pupa*, doll, girl) a figure moved by a wire in a mock drama.

Puppet-player. One that manages the motions of a puppet.

Puppet-show. A mock drama performed with puppets moved by wire.

In this morass of words one can see a gleam of truth. I suppose it is an affectation of the puppet to pretend to portray the emotions of human conduct. The little men of Lilliput aping the manners of Brobdingnag, but in this very aping lie the lessons of puppetry, for puppetry can and does reveal not only the fun of life but the foibles of the human kind also. Upon reflection, I like that definition of puppetry. It strikes near the truth. A puppet, the dictionary tells us, bears its name derived from *pupa*, a doll or a girl. The marionette derives its name, it is believed, from a corruption of *mariolette*—

little Mary. This is a reference to The Blessed Virgin Mary, for early marionette shows depicted The Nativity and the scenes enacted around The Crib.

The emphasis within the definition that a puppet is manipulated by a *wire*, or by *wires*, suggests a much older beginning than even the *mariolette*. The primitive puppets were and still are manipulated by a rod and the modern rod-puppet is an adaptation of this ancient form.

Yet another authority gives the origin of the term marionette as derivation from *morio*, an Italian word meaning " a fool or a buffoon." Still another associates it with the name of Marion, an Italian who brought puppets from Italy into France during the reign of Charles IX. Italy had long known the fun of the puppet under the name of *fantoccini*.

For my part I am at the moment content to accept the antiquity of the puppet and to assign the derivation of the term marionette to *mariolette*. It seems consistent with the vital part played by the Church in early dramatic art.

In Egypt the jointed puppet was well known. Recent excavations among the tombs of Ancient Egypt bring more and more of these marvellous little fellows once again into the light of day. Philosophically we may muse upon these diminutive creatures. They played before the great of ancient times. Then they lay in the darkness of the sealed tomb for centuries. Then once again they reappear. The world has changed. The puppet has not changed. He still struts the stage with jerking stride, telling the same stories. Only the names and the idiomatic language have changed.

Greece, too, knew her puppets and one puppet-player, yclept Potheinos, rose to great popularity because of his puppets and their plays.

India had her puppets centuries ago. Some authorities believe that since India was the home of the fairy-tale she might also be the home and origin of the puppet plays.

" In the collection of Kashmiri tales compiled from ancient sources by the eleventh-century writer, Somadeva, there is mention of mechanical puppets worked by means of a wooden peg ; some flew in the air, brought water, danced, and even spoke. Others were worked by string, the operator being known as the *Sutradhar* (string-puller). This word is still applied to a stage manager, a fact suggesting that the puppet play was the earliest form of stage exhibition." (Vide, *The British Encyclopædia*.)

It is believed that Persia gained her knowledge of puppets from India, for there was free passage in those days. The puppet moved onwards to the Far East and to Java.

In *The Handbook to the Ethnographical Collections* (British Museum), one may read concerning Java :

" As regards amusements, the institution which claims first mention is the Javanese Wayang. This is a puppet show and is divided into three classes : the Wayang purwa, the Wayang gedog, and the Wayang klitik. The first deals with the earliest period of Javanese and Hindu mythological history, the last with the latest period of history down to the destruction of the Kingdom of Majapahit. The first two forms of Wayang are shadow plays, the puppets being cut from leather ; in the last, however, they are carved from wood. Appropriate comments are recited by the owner of the show, called Dalang in archaic language, to the accompaniment of an orchestra composed of gongs and xylophones."

That takes us a long way back in terms of antiquity.

From the East we find the puppet marching forward steadily towards Europe. The gypsies brought him as they brought so much that was fine across the world. One day, perhaps, someone will arise who will write a book showing the debt civilisation owes to the wandering tribes of gypsies. It has become the custom to deride these wanderers, to call them rogues and horse thieves, undesirable folk living wild upon the fringe of civilisation. That is a lie, but it is a lie which will die hard. It will die, however, yet in the way of things it may mean that the gypsy tribes will have to die out first. Then we shall get tomes of commendation where now we get tornadoes of abuse.

It is recorded that in the year 1812, an English traveller, Ouseley by name, saw a gypsy show in Tabriz. But 1812 is almost recent history. It was the gypsies who performed the sacred stories of Christmas and Lent in Moldavia. It was the gypsies who adapted the puppet show to a news-reel of the Russo-Turkish War, telling the audience of the latest bulletins. If in the final fight between a Russian and a Turk, the Russian won, the audience knew that there was news of a Russian victory. If the Turk overcame the Cossack then a Turkish gain was recorded.

May not our news-reels have their roots in the past also ? Are they quite as modern as we believe them to be ?

The gypsies, however, were not the only puppeteers. Others arose to carry on the art. These were largely ill-educated men, just as our early schools were conducted by ill-educated folk.

In France, Jean Brioché, a tooth drawer, performed with puppets under Louis XIV. Brioché possessed a lively monkey graced by the name of Fagotin. Brioché, Fagotin and his company of puppets were extremely popular.

In Germany, a tailor named Reibehand grew to fame with *his* puppet show.

Samuel Pepys wites in his *Diary :*

" At the office all the morning ; and at noon my wife and Deb and Mercer and W. Hewer and I to the Fair and there, at the old house, did eat a pig, and was pretty merry, but saw no sights, my wife having a mind to see the play *Bartholomew Fair* with puppets. And it is an excellent play, the more I see it, the more I love the wit of it ; only the business of abusing the Puritans begins to grow stale and of no use, they being the people that at last, will be found the wisest."

So puppets were well established in Stuart times and we know that they had been in England anyway since the time of Chaucer.

Once in England the puppet took root. Punch and Judy is our finest traditional example, and who is there " with soul so dead " who can see a Punch and Judy show and not grow excited ? If such a being live, then let him be drummed out ceremonially from the company of all good men and true.

So down the ages until to-day, when we have the British Puppet and Model Theatre Guild, welding together the puppeteers of England, visiting countries abroad and establishing links which will lead more surely to an international society than all the edicts, protocols, all the treaties of the politicians.

The puppet laughs at foibles and in that laughter all men find their kindred.

CHAPTER TEN

I HAVE no desire to emphasise that if one takes up puppetry one must learn a good deal. So much must be obvious to all. Puppetry is an art and it is also a craft and no one can paint a picture of create a new form without acquiring a new skill through the new experience.

But I do not emphasise this, for to do so would be to reduce puppetry to the level of a moral lesson, the most loathsome thing in the curriculum of the school. If every lesson is not in itself a moral lesson, then lessons specially labelled as " moral " will be worse than useless.

What I do wish to point out, however, is that through puppetry one may enter many new fields, all of which are interesting, some profitable in a material sense.

Let us examine the ramifications of puppetry for a moment to see how far I can uphold my assertion.

You wish to make a puppet. You start. You want to know the proportions of the figure. How much of the total height of the figure is occupied by the head ? How many heads-high is a fully adult and well-proportioned figure ? How far down the thighs should come the tips of the fingers ? How far up the total length of the body should the waist appear ? Where between hip and ankle should the knee appear ?

These questions must be answered. To find that answer you must study proportion, the proportion of the human figure.

You have made your puppet. Now it must be dressed. In the dressing of the puppet you get to learn something

of the *line* of dress designing and quite a lot about colour
and design in dress.

Then you must build your theatre.   It must be painted.
The scenes must be designed and decorated.   The
curtains must exactly suit the play.   Here are art and
design and colour and creation.

You will want to know something of historical costume,
for you may want to give a " period play."   That means
you will have to search for plates in books on costume
and here you find yourself in the world of History.

Then on the much more material side you grow skilful
in measurement and in calculation   All very good fun
and excellent training for all of us.

Suppose you wish to write a play.   You must know
the period in which you set your play or you will insert
anachronisms which may ruin your play before a critical
audience.   Costume, language, custom, invention, these
must be correctly placed.

You cannot awaken Alfred the Great with an alarm
clock any more than you can make the Bright Young
Things of the pre-war period say " Definitely " and
" Devastating," which words belong to the Bright Young
Things of the post-war period, almost post-post-war at
that !

You cannot make Queen Victoria say " Not bloody
likely " to one of her Cabinet Ministers, but a modern
grandmother may say so, because now the word is dull
and respectable, through constant usage, and we have
not the imagination to create new curses.   The eighteenth
century seems to have crabbed that market for us.

Keep as far as is humanly possible within the period,
allowing no anachronisms.   You cannot be absolutely
faultless in this.   Life moves so rapidly.   But you can
prevent glaring examples which may ruin your play.

Your play.   Music.   You must choose your incidental
music with care and discrimination.   Music can create

the atmosphere for the play. It can also ruin the play. Can you imagine the sensation you would cause if you played Stanley Holloway's song, " With her head tucked underneath her arm," as the prelude to Hamlet ? The song runs to its end. The curtain goes back. " Who's there ? " snaps Bernado, and before the answer can come every member of the audience is seeing the vision of the poor decapitated lady—and waiting for her to appear— with her head tucked underneath her arm. And then Francisco enters . . .

No. You must be as careful in your choice of music as you must be in the choice of dress and design and of colour.

Once you begin puppetry you find yourself in a fascinating world which embraces almost all cultural activities. That is the power and the fun of puppetry.

NEMO

A Phantasy of Life .. in One Act

By

ARTHUR B. ALLEN

First performed by The British Model Theatre
Guild in 1930

Characters : THE MAN
THE TREE-THAT-TALKS
THE GRASS
THE NETTLES
THE WIND
PAN

TIME.—*At the end of the day when the daylight merges
into night and neither holds supreme. At the time of
day when one is prone to dreams and fancies, when the
earth is falling asleep and when man feels the tie which
binds him to nature.*

THE SETTING.—*A small glade in a wood. Across
this open space there lies an old tree trunk. All around
there tower trees of several sizes and species. But all
the trees are symbols, and* THE GRASS *and* THE NETTLES
*are symbolised. Each growth is enlarged so that the
blades of grass are as tall as a man, and the nettles reach
above his head. A clump of* GRASS *lies to the right, while*
THE TREE-THAT-TALKS *lies to the left centre.* THE
NETTLES *are to the extreme left and* THE MAN *is discovered seated right centre. He sits upon the tree trunk.
He is dejected, has been wandering about until forced
to rest through sheer exhaustion.*

THE MAN : This is the end. Loved . . . and lost.
Down in a hole in the ground . . . cold . . . wet.
Lonely . . . Lonely like I am.
Wonder if she tries to reach me—as I try to reach
her ?
No. She's dead . . . gone right away. Just went
out like a flame into the darkness.

I wish I believed in—Heaven. I could perhaps
rest then. I can see her there—in Heaven.
No . . . no . . . that's sacrilege. She's too good
for Heaven, for any Heaven. She died like a
flower dies, and there is no Heaven for flowers,
they tell us.
There's nothing . . . and she's gone to nothing.
(*A bird breaks into song somewhere in the tree-tops.*
THE MAN *listens carefully, brightening at first, cheered
by the song, but the depression settles again.*)
THE MAN : Ah! Sing away, sing away. Soon you'll
be dead.
Cold . . . like she is. Cold . . . no song, no life,
just dead.
Six months I knew her . . . one month married.
I can see her now, the morning when we met.
There was gossamer and dew, and a crimson morn-
ing light. There was a tang in the air and we
talked. Not much . . . not much. We thought
and felt. We were so much together, so truly
one. There was no need to talk . . . no need
to talk . . . only to think.
Think! (*He laughs and it jars.*)
Now she can't think. She's dead.
A month we were married. We two made one.
One . . . One . . . the one is broken. After a
month of life then nothing.
There was no hope from the first. A broken cart
shaft leaves no hope in a body. Curse that
driver! May he rot! Yet how could he help
it? It was not his fault really. How should
he know we were to skid?
God! I feel it now. The windscreen gone, she
cried, I turned. She was pinned by that shaft,
pinned, like a singing bird on a blackthorn.
I see her now . . . white . . . still.

Still. (*A whisper.*)

O God! Let me forget! Let me forget!

She's dead . . . and I'm alone.

She's cold . . . and I'm at fever heat.

She is going into dust . . . and I live in torment.

It is the end . . . the end of all things.

(THE MAN *breaks down, burying his head in his hands. The silence is intense, broken by an occasional dry sob. Almost imperceptibly there comes the sound of the rustling of grasses and the passing of the wind in the tree-tops. An occasional bird is heard to sing, the silence falls. The wind passes over the glade, making a quiet sigh among the foliage. The leaves skirl for a moment and then fall inert again.* THE MAN *looks up as if drawn by a power greater than his despondency. He gazes around as if he has heard a voice, but seeing nothing, sinks again into his semi-comatic state. He stares at the audience with unseeing eyes, and mutters occasionally to himself. Then he starts and remains rigid.*)

THE TREE-THAT-TALKS : There is no end.

THE MAN : Who spoke? Who's there? (*He jumps up wildly, looking round. Then he laughs and sits down.*)
No one. No one. I could have sworn I heard a voice. I must be going mad. Mad . . . Mad. That's it. I'm going mad. (*He laughs again.*) I'm hearing voices . . . Who cares? Perhaps I shan't remember . . . if I'm mad.

THE TREE : There is no such thing as madness. Some have ears that hear and some are without hearing. Some have eyes that see and some are without sight. You have ears that hear and eyes that see. My voice you heard when I said to you : "There is no end." I say again to you there is no end. For that which has no beginning can have no end. Turn your eyes within you and you shall see the meaning written therein.

THE MAN: What the devil . . . ! Who the hell *are* you ?

THE TREE: I am the Tree.

THE MAN: Tree ? Tree ? Then I am mad.

THE TREE: Not mad, only frightened.

THE MAN: Frightened ? Huh ! What the devil have I to be frightened about ? Nothing. Nothing. (*In a whisper.*)

THE TREE: Nothing to be frightened about ?

THE MAN: No, nothing. (*Vehemently as if to convince himself.*)

THE TREE: Not even a life alone ?

THE MAN: Damn you !

THE TREE: You are frightened of yourself, frightened of all that's in you, frightened of life.

THE MAN: I tell you no !

THE TREE: Yet it is so. (*A pause.*)

THE MAN: Yet it is so. (*Slowly.*)

THE TREE: You have had a loss.

THE MAN: Who are you ? (*Frightened.*)

THE TREE: I am the Tree.

THE MAN: Mad. Mad. Stark, raving mad. How do you know what you know ?

THE TREE: I am the Tree of Knowledge. I know all.

THE MAN: Tree of Knowledge ? That was in Eden. Is this Eden ? Am I translated ? Adam regenerate ? I'm hearing things. I'd better go.

THE TREE: You cannot go.

THE MAN (*tries to leave the spot but finds he cannot*) : Why is this ? Why can't I go ? What has happened ?

THE TREE: You are under the spell of your imaginings. Many a time have you tried to face yourself and get things thrashed out. Now you have gone too far to turn back. You are held by your imaginings.

THE MAN: The spell of imagination !

THE TREE : By your imagination can you see where no eye sees ?

THE MAN : That's the curse of it. I see too much. I can see here, there——

THE TREE : And not enough. You see as far as the gate, but you do not take the step forward and look over the top bar. All men gifted with imagination are cowards.

THE MAN : Am I a coward ?

THE TREE : Craven. But you are as other men.

THE MAN : Craven ?

THE TREE : You are alone now—now she has gone from you.

THE MAN : She's dead. You awake my memory, when I want to forget.

THE TREE : Memory and Imagination are fellows. They travel together in all normal men. You are mistaken, for she is not dead.

THE MAN : Not dead ? Not dead ? You're a fool whatever you are ! I saw her die. She died in my arms. I held her dead. I saw her buried . . . two days now. Two days buried and you say she isn't dead. Fool ! Fool ! You're mad . . . like I am. Damn you ! Why do you torture me ?

THE TREE : I come to heal you. You torture yourself.

THE MAN : Torture myself ? Yes. Perhaps I do.

THE TREE : She is not dead. She is out of man's reach. *But she lives.*

THE MAN : Is she then a spirit ?

THE TREE : What have we to do with spirits, or spirits with us ? These are but the eddies of an overwrought mind . . . the fruits of fear. The desire for immortality when naught is immortal but the mind. Were she a spirit, how would that please you ? Could you reach her ? Could you go ? Could you fold her in your arms ? Love her ?

THE MAN : For God's sake, stop !

THE TREE : Desiring to be near her you put her farther out of reach. Madman ! But she is near you, around you, by you, waiting for you if you will come.

THE MAN : Eh ?

THE TREE : Seek your answer among the Nettles. You will find it true.

THE NETTLES : You need not speak, we know your thoughts. It's true. Why should you doubt the Tree ? She is sleeping. But in her sleep she grows towards you, you who made her whole.

THE TREE : Seek among the blades of Grass, they will tell you too.

THE GRASS : It is so. She sleeps like the Sleeping Beauty. Soon shall the sun's rays kiss her and she will awaken. Will you not be there to receive her ? Or shall she seek in vain ?

THE TREE : Let the Wind speak.

THE WIND : It is true. I who see all, hear all, play with all, say that this is so.

THE MAN : How ? How ? Oh, God, tell me ? I saw her die I tell you . . . saw her buried. Where is she if she isn't dead ? Take me to her ! Take me to her !

(*A pause.*)

THE TREE : Her breath is in the wind.

THE WIND : And her rhythm in the swaying tree-tops.

THE TREE : Her blush is in the dawn's light.

THE GRASS : And the sparkle of her eye in the dew.

THE WIND : Her laughter is in the brook's song.

THE NETTLES : And her strength in the mighty oak.

THE GRASS : The white of her sinews in the nettles' roots.

THE WIND : And her love in the slender vine.

THE TREE : Her song is in the bird's throat.

THE GRASS : Her whisper among the sedges.

THE NETTLES : Her fleetness is in the deer's foot.

THE TREE : The glint of her hair in the sea.

THE GRASS : Her moods are in the spring-time.

THE NETTLES : And her faith in the light of the moon.

THE WIND : Her caresses are found in the twilight.

THE TREE : Her tears in the April showers.

PAN (*suddenly appearing from behind* THE TREE) : And she is here with you and us. And so you'll find, my forlorn, despondent friend, what is, is, and cannot be broken. She will not appear as heretofore. So go your way, your youth is with you. See her where she is. She is alive, throbbing, loving. She is of us, in us. Go seek her, my son, for one day you, too, will return to me who gave you birth that you might return again to me who am all life. Go seek her. Go in peace.

THE TREE : Peace.

THE GRASS : Go—

THE NETTLES : In—

THE WIND : Peace.

(PAN *disappears behind* THE TREE. THE WIND *passes by with a bold embracing. The notes of birds are heard.* THE MAN *awakens as if from a dream.*)

THE MAN : What ? Who spoke ? (*He gets up and looks round.*) I'll swear I heard a voice. But I'm all alone. No . . . no, I'm not. I've got all the things that matter. I've got youth and health, and nature. She was so fond of nature, too. The wind in her hair, the frost-glow on her cheeks, her breath whitening in the air. Why didn't I think of all this before ? I've been a fool. But I'm awake now. God ! How I miss her, but I'll fight and live as she would have me live.

(*He stands for a moment or two as if in thought or listening to a voice, silent to all save him alone. Then bracing his shoulders he slowly leaves the woods, to face the world alone.*)

AND THE CURTAIN FALLS.

PUPPETRY FOR BEGINNERS

STAGE TWO

CHAPTER ONE

THE PUPPET FAMILY

WE grow so used to thinking of the puppet family in terms of :
(a) Cut-outs
(b) Glove puppets
(c) Jointed puppets or marionettes
that sometimes we grow careless of subdivisions.

The cut-out figures may be straight cut-outs, perfectly flat without any device added for the introduction of movement. But cut-out figures may also move, the movement being introduced upon the *Jumping-Jack principle*.

Cut-out figures may also be made transparent so that colour can be introduced into the shadow-show. I have dealt with this idea of cut-out transparencies elsewhere. I shall develop the Jumping-Jack later in this particular book.

Glove puppets in the normal run of activity operate only in so far as the two fingers and thumb on any one hand can introduce movement. But it is possible by a simple manipulation of strings to develop other motions.

For example, suppose it is necessary for a glove puppet to pick up a pail and take it from one side of the stage to the other, it can do so by hooking the handle of the pail over its hand. But that presupposes that the handle of the pail is standing in an upright position. Now in the general run of things the handle of a pail does *not* stand upright. It lies down. So the handle must be raised and it must-be raised realistically. A string fastened to the centre of the handle and reaching up into the " flies " of the theatre will allow you to raise the handle as and when the motions of the puppet require raising. The puppet can then hook his fist through the handle and move the pail from position 1 into position 2.

All action in glove puppetry independent of hand movement may be introduced by string manipulation.

A word of warning here. Do not overdo this auxiliary move-ment. I know it looks clever, but too much cleverness in puppetry spoils the whole show. You are not training to be a trick merchant, a super-illusionist. You are training to be an honest puppeteer pre-senting an honest show. Eschew flashy tricks as you would the devil.

FIG. 1.

So puppets are not only divided into the three groups—cut-outs, glove and marionettes—they are subdivided too. And these subdivisions among others may be classified in terms of operation and, or, movement.

In terms of *shape*, puppets may be grouped into two classes. They are either *flat* or they are *round*. That is, they are designed either upon a two-dimensional plan or upon a three-dimensional plan. If you cut a figure from a picture, mount it upon cardboard and operate by introducing the figure at the end of a stick or a wire from one or other of the wings, then you are presenting a flat puppet, a puppet in two dimensions. (*Fig. 1.*) If, however, you make a jointed puppet that moves and has the natural proportions of the human figure (even though such proportions may be caricatured), then you present a three-dimensional puppet. (*Fig. 2.*)

FIG. 2.

So puppets are either :

(*a*) Flat ; or

(*b*) Round.

If we examine carefully the family of *flat puppets* we find a further subdivision, a succession of cousins by marriage, as it were.

The *cut-out*, generally speaking, covers all forms of flat puppets. These may be constructed out of thick paper, cardboard, three-ply, composition board (e.g., Beaver Board, SX Board, Lloyd Board, or Tough Board). If you use three-ply or the thick composition pulp boards then you will have to cut out your figures, using a fretsaw.

In terms of operation you may manipulate a cut-out figure :

(*a*) from above, that is by means of a slender rod projecting down from the " flies " to the head of the figure ; or

(*b*) from below the stage, again using a slender rod which is fastened either to the legs, to one leg, or to the body of the figure , or

(*c*) from stage level, by fastening the figure to a rod or wire and introducing the figure on to the stage from either left or right or right to left of the stage, as the action of the play requires.

Do not forget that in some types of play presentation it may be necessary to move your cut-out figures, not only *across* the stage, but also from the back of the stage to the front, and from front to the back. I had such a need while producing my own dramatic version of the Russian folk tale, *The Golden Cock*. I tried inserting the rods through the base of the backcloth, joining the rods to the figures at right angles to the figures. This answered only as and when I wished to move forwards and backwards, making a character or a group of characters advance or retire upon the stage.

But since I also wanted to move these same figures not only forwards and backwards but *also* across the stage, I found the front and back technique impossible. So by dint of careful practice I was able to advance or retreat my characters *from the wings*. The problem is really simple enough. It means that you must learn to keep the rod projecting from the wings parallel to the

front of the stage throughout the whole movement. Therefore, you *must* see that the stage floor is smooth and free
from all catchpoints.   See, too, that the base of the rod
is sandpapered to smoothness.   Nothing catches so
easily as a rough-cut piece of timber.   It grabs like a
grappling iron and holds on just as effectively.   You can
ruin a whole show by allowing rough
edges to remain.   Which is absurd
when you consider that a few strokes
of sandpaper will prevent the whole
trouble.

So flat figures in puppetry may be
manipulated :

(*a*) From above the stage. (*Fig.* 3.)
(*b*) From below the stage. (*Fig.* 4.)
(*c*) From stage level. (*Fig.* 5.)

The same principles apply, of
course, to shadow shows, which are
at their best when cut-out figures
are used.   I have seen shadow shows
presented where the producer has
used his three-dimensional puppets.
But I do not like them and I do not
recommend such a technique.   For
one thing the strings of the puppets
show upon the shadow screen.   This
is not so very annoying when the

FIG. 3.
Cut-out operated from
above the stage.

strings are kept *taut*, but in stringed puppetry some
strings sag when not in use.   This is quite natural when
all is said and done, the strings must sag.   The shadow
shows the sagging string, then that limb is to be moved
and the audience knows that that limb will move in a
moment, for it sees the tightening up of the string *first
of all*.   Thus the essential illusion is destroyed.

No, leave three-dimensional puppets out of your
shadow shows—use cut-outs only.

In the shadow show it is inadvisable to operate your figures from above, it kills the illusion. You may operate your figures from below the stage either by a rod or wire, or by rod and string. The rod then controls the main movement and the string introduces the auxiliary movement.

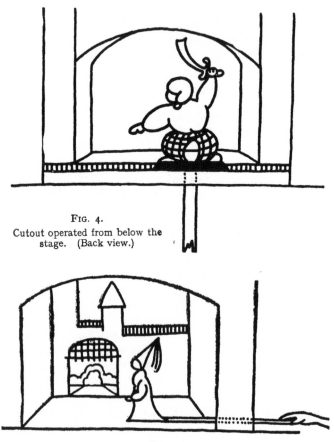

FIG. 4.
Cutout operated from below the stage. (Back view.)

FIG. 5.
Cut-out operated from stage level.

Again quoting from experience : if auxiliary action *is* required then I prefer to introduce the cut-out from the wings, and leave the auxiliary action to be introduced into the character by the manipulation of a string from below the stage.

For example, suppose you are producing *Dick Whittington*. (Fig. 6.)

FIG. 6.

The scene opens with only the milestone showing. The milestone is a solid shadow, but letters and the figures giving the distance yet to be walked to London are transparencies. They have been cut out carefully, backed by greaseproof paper so that the legend upon the stone is just perceivable—and readable—by the audience.

F

FIG. 7.

The Cat enters from the left. Stops by the milestone, remains there. Perhaps for a moment it soliloquises and carries on the story pending the arrival at the stone of Dick Whittington himself. Dick enters from the right. He comes forward slowly, wearily. He carries his bundle over his shoulder tied to the end of his staff. He, too, stops by the stone. He stops on the side farthest away from the Cat. He *is* weary. He raises the stick and bundle from off his shoulder, brings it right over until stick and bundle rest upon the ground before him. (*Fig. 7.*) This means that Dick's arm, the stick and the bundle are all in one piece. A string pulled from below the stage pulls that limb into action.

Dick stands and talks to the Cat. They decide to go on together. A second string is pulled. The arm, stick

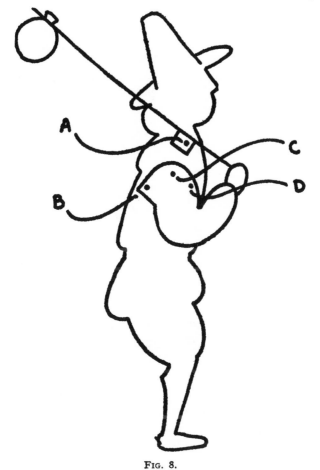

FIG. 8.

and bundle rise, go through the full arc and finally rest into position 1. The bundle once more is behind Dick, the stave upon his shoulder. (*Fig. 8.*)

I saw this enacted in Moscow. The Cat was moulded upon a circular base, mounted upon a wire rod. The circular base was in effect two wooden discs. The lower disc was fastened firmly to the rod. The upper disc swivelled in the centre. When Dick and the Cat decided to go off together, a string operated from the wings operated the upper disc. The Cat turned about and walked off quite naturally—not backwards. You might consider the possible development of the swivelling of the figures. (*Fig.* 9.)

FIG. 9.

Swivel base. Top circle movable. Operated by a
string wound around the upper stand. Lower stand
fastened to operating rod.

But take care that the movable parts are neither too loose nor too tight. You keep control of the base by a purchase upon the guiding rod.

In some shadow plays you may operate your figures from either :

(*a*) below the stage (*Fig.* 10), or

(*b*) from the wings (*Fig.* 11),

and shadow figures may be either ·

(*a*) solid figures casting an opaque shadow (*Fig.* 12), or

FIG. 10.

Shadow show operated from behind a below stage. Showing
the position of the operators.

Fig. 11.

Shadow show, with figure introduced from the wings.

Fig. 12.

Shadow show seen from the front.

(*b*) transparent figures introducing colour (*Fig.* 13).

So much then for the flat figure families. We come now to the rotund. Puppets in the round, the three-dimensional figures, include :

(*a*) The marionettes, the string figures which ape the gestures of humanity.

(*b*) The glove puppets.

(*c*) The rod puppets.

FIG. 13.

Transparency. Cut-outs all area between the remaining framework fasten coloured cellophane, or coloured paper.

The marionette is operated from above the stage, the doll hanging from the controls upon manipulation strings.

Glove puppets are worked from below the stage, the figure cloaking the hand that controls its action.

The rod puppet may be operated from above or from below. Here I exclude the cut-out figure which is, of course. a form of rod puppet, but of two dimensions and not three.

The analysis of the puppet family in terms of its manipulation forces you into an immediate decision. As and when you plan your puppet production, deciding upon the type of puppet you are to employ, you must decide *at once* upon the stage decoration and arrangement. You must have nothing upon the stage that will interfere in any way with the free movement of the figures.

When producing with marionettes you can, of course, make them walk around the furniture, as a human actor may, but with rod puppets and with cut-outs in particular, keep the stage clear of all *impedimenta*. The rigidity and conservatism of movement in both rod and cut-out types demand a clear stage.

CHAPTER TWO

JUMPING-JACK PUPPETS

EXCEPT as a trick of the stage there is little place for the Jumping-Jack puppet. This form is useful when you are staging a solo turn in the nature of a song-and-dance show. Here you are depending upon the *spectacle* instead of upon the *story*. Not a wise proceeding at all in puppetry. However, since a little vice makes virtue appear the more virtuous, I see no reason why, once in a way, you should not depart from the straight and narrow and have a little flutter on your own!

Just once in a while, and cleanse your soul of a too cramping rectitude, as it were.

So, despite the blows I know will fall upon my shoulders from the purists among puppeteers—here goes. The irony of the situation lies in the fact that I have always regarded myself as among that select company of puritans. There was once, however, a revolt in Heaven and I am certain sure it was because Lucifer grew a little weary of wearing a halo and wanted to play ball with it for a day or two. In which case Jehovah showed a sad lacking in humour. What Lucifer so obviously wanted was leave of absence to play whoopee. Given that, he would have become, no doubt, the perfect angel. It is interesting to reflect that the modern psychologist would have diagnosed his trouble immediately and have prescribed for Lucifer an extra ration of barley sugar. Then the rebellious spirit of the sugar-stick-sucking Satan would have been quietened and all would have been well in

Heaven. But perhaps psychologists do not go to Heaven. . . .

A Jumping-Jack is no more, no less, than a cut-out figure, jointed and strung. The Jumping-Jack is by Cut-out, out of Marionette, with the bar sinister blazing from his escutcheon. . . .

The Jumping-Jack is considered, by pure puppeteers, as being not quite respectable.

No matter. The Jumping-Jack is fun. Puppetry is fun, and if " by indirections we find directions out," who shall be the poorer or sadder ? Neither you nor I. At least we shall have had our fun together. . . .

I feel here that a drawing can do more than mere words, so turn to my drawing of the Jumping-Jack. Here you will see how to string the little fellow and how to use him. You will at once notice, I am sure, an adaptation that is needed when the Jumping-Jack enters a model theatre. (*Fig.* 14.)

In the ordinary course of usage, you hold the Jumping-Jack by a string attached to his head and you operate his movements from *below*.

While this *is* possible in a model theatre, it is not advisable. It is better to mount the Jack upon a vertical stick, colour that stick a self-colour to the surrounding hue and hold and operate from below. This will necessitate a groove cut *across* the stage floor of sufficient width to allow the free passage of the supporting rod. Thus the Jumping-Jack joins the category of puppets worked from below. He is also of the *genus*, the flat puppet.

When in Russia I saw a very ingenious arrangement of Jumping-Jack figures. It was a chorus scene. The principals in the drama were stringed puppets, acting on the stage in the traditional manner. Behind them, mounted upon four tiers and forming a living pyramid of chorus girls, were the Jumping-Jack figures. They were

FIG. 14.
The Jumping Jack. "A" front view.

FIG. 14.
The Jumping Jack. " B " back view showing stringing.

beautifully dressed in frilly frocks; they performed in
perfect time the stereotyped high jinks of the chorus.

Intrigued by the precision of this chorus I went behind
stage to discover if I could how this was done. I found
out how this was done and it was quite simple—once you
knew how. The chorus was, as I say, arranged in a
pyramid. Thus:

```
                    X
            X               X
        X           X               X
    X           X           X               X
```

Each limb was operated separately. Thus all left legs
were operated by single strings running down from the
puppet to beneath the stage. Each string was fastened
to a wire " key," a straight piece of wire running from
a fixed board under the stage towards the operator. All
these separate keys were linked up to a single board, so
that by depressing the left leg key-board, all the left legs
arose simultaneously. The right legs were linked up in a
like manner. Thus by depressing the key-boards alter-
nately the limbs rose harmoniously. By depressing both
key-boards at once the chorus gave an exhibition of
" aerial splits." This, however, was the finale and not
exercised without due restraint.

The figures themselves were held upright by pieces of
galvanised wire painted in the same tone as the backcloth and so rendered almost invisible.

It is because I have this spectacle so vividly in mind
that I have ventured to dare the wrath of the purist and
written of the Jumping-Jack in this work on simple
puppetry.

CHAPTER THREE

ONE of the most successful puppet shows I ever saw was given by a class of boys in a poor school. It *was* a poor school, not only in the building, but among the parents of those children, scarcely one square meal was to be found.

Yet, fired by the desire to make their own puppets and to present their own puppet plays, the boys got together and made their figures out of broomsticks and dowel rods.

Is there not here an inspiration for all of us ? Is there not here a salutary lesson to those of us who have felt that we must have a collection of perfectly modelled puppets before we *dare* begin upon our work ?

These lads, fired by enthusiasm, determined to succeed, using broom staves and dowel rods and little pieces of aged rags where others require extravagant costumes and tinsel and sequins ! How did they do it ? Quite simply.

A broom stave cut into four-inch lengths. This made the body of the puppet. The heads were crudely carved, it is true, but carved they were from large lumps of wood. The arms and legs were from dowel rods of two thicknesses, the thinner rods for the arms, the thicker for the legs. The hands they made of little pieces of firewood carved with a penknife.

If you turn now to my illustration (*Fig.* 15) you will see how it was done. Why not make a start here if you feel a little nervous of beginning a more ambitious programme ?

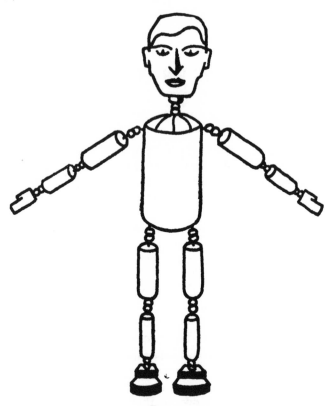

FIG. 15.
Broomstick and Dowel Puppet.

CHAPTER FOUR

A SIMPLE JOINTED PUPPET

HERE is another form of jointed puppet which anyone can make.

First you make the head out of plastic wood or Barbola. Model the head first as a tapering, but not too tapering, " egg." Allow for the neck during the modelling. Add eyes separately, add nose separately, if you cannot model from from the mass. The ears do not want to protrude very far from the side of the head so it should be possible for you to model from the solid. Just indicate where the ears should be.

The body is a flat block of wood, separated at the pelvic girdle. So the body is in reality two pieces of wood, one large and one small. They are joined by two small screw-eyes interlocked. To interlock screw-eyes, open one with a pair of pliers. Hook the second unopened screw-eye into the first and then close up the opened screw-eye. They are now interlocked and there is a wealth of " play " between the two screws.

The larger of the two pieces of wood you can leave square-cut or you can cut away each side a little so that the trunk tapers to the waist. This I shall leave to you. It is after all a matter of personal preference.

For the thighs use fairly thick dowel rods. For the shins use a narrower gauge in dowel rods. Fasten thighs to the pelvic girdle with two interlocked screw-eyes. Fasten the shins to the thighs with two interlocking screw-eyes. The feet you can carve out of firewood. If you use firewood for this, remember that the feet will be very light in weight. Light feet on a puppet are a nuisance. They refuse to hang correctly and when you try to make the puppet *walk* there is a marked tendency for the puppet to exhibit all the unfortunate symptoms of St. Vitus' Dance. So if you do use firewood, sole the feet with lead sheeting.

Better still, carve the feet in wood and then make a plaster cast mould and cast the feet in lead. One can always find odd lengths of lead piping lying around the house. Use these odd lengths, they serve admirably.

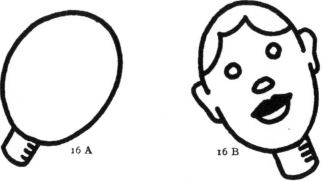

16 A   16 B

FIG. 16   A—B.
A—Beginning of the head.   B—Finished head.

A puppeteer should always keep an oddments box into which go all pieces of lead, pieces of wire, screw-eyes and such knick-knacks which may come in useful one day. This is not hoarding junk. It is being far sighted.

You have now to make the hands and arms. From shoulder to elbow use thick string. Put a screw-eye into the shoulder. Put another screw-eye into the forearm. Thread the string through the eyes. Fray the ends, moisten with seccotine. Put frayed end to frayed end and roll carefully between the thumb and forefinger. This will intermingle the frayed fringes and the seccotine will cement the join.

The forearms are made of dowel rods of the same gauge as you made the shins. The hands you can carve from firewood.

Now turn to my illustration (*Fig.* 16) and you will see this figure as it looks standing " in the buff."

C 16

16 D

FIG. 16 C—D
C—Foot. D—Hand.

G

CHAPTER FIVE

HOW TO MAKE A PUPPET HEAD

A GLOVE puppet must have a head, and the head of the glove puppet must have striking characteristics.

Remember Punch's head in Punch and Judy ? You would know it anywhere. I saw a Punch and Judy show in a school in Russia. I understood no word of the language, but there was no mistaking the character.

So when modelling a head for a glove puppet aim for character. Make the *face* tell its own story. The Mad Hatter, in *Alice in Wonderland*, is easily recognisable because of the hat ! But if you are creating a Miser, make it a miserly face. Make that face show all the meanness, all the avarice, all the treachery that are the characteristics of so foul a type.

If you wish to portray Hodge, the stupid yokel, make his face as daft as his action. Give him a vacant look in a rubicon face. Give him straws in his hay-wire hair and crown him with a billycock hat. Dress him in a smock and there you are. . . .

Create character.

Add nothing that detracts from the character. Remember the pert reply : " ' My face is my fortune, sir,' she said "—and act upon it. And if some of the faces you make would bankrupt their owner, do not despair. You will get a world of fun out of your trials and errors and that will be worth something. Puppetry is an ancient and honourable craft. It did not grow up overnight. So keep a brave heart and experiment on.

Now how shall we begin to make a head ? Remember the head is for a glove puppet. A quick sure-fire method of making a head for a glove puppet, one method out of many. Yet an effective and efficient method :

1. Get a newspaper and soak in water until you can pinch and model it into any shape. Be careful that the paper does not pulp, as it will do if you keep it in water too long.

2. Take the paper out of the water. Squeeze the surplus water from the paper. Tear several strips from the soaked sheet. Bind these round and round your index finger until you have a knob of paper at the end of your finger. Pinch and squeeze this knob into an oval shape about as big as you wish the finished head to be.

3. Tear some tissue paper into strips and using Gloy, Lap, or ordinary flour paste cover the strips with the adhesive. Well cover the strips.

4. Bind these strips round and round the egg-shaped pulp " knob " until the whole of the surface area is covered and bound. Here is your head base.

5. Now bind more strips to make the projections of forehead and cranium. Keep in mind that a human head does *not* as a general rule go straight down from back of the head to the back of the neck. The skull protrudes beyond the plane of the neck projected upwards. The additional strips will produce these protuberances.

6. When you were pinching the soaked paper into the basic shape you will, of course, have allowed somewhat for the neck. Bind the tissue strips around this crude neck so that you get a smooth tubular effect. You can leave the neck at this stage, for much will be covered by the costume.

7. The cheekbones will want padding out. The nose raised from the plane of the face. The eyebrows, too, ears, lips, the chin, all these are *raised* areas and are now modelled on to the base. Use the tissue strips and

adhesive, and model carefully, using thumb and forefinger as modelling tools.

8. Now stand to dry. This standing to dry constitutes a difficulty, for if the wet head falls upon a hard surface it will be damaged. That is obvious !

FIG. 17.

I have found that a block of plasticene or a box filled with tight-packed damp earth is a great help here.

Place the head carefully upon the blunted end of a wooden skewer and jab the pointed end into the clay or earth. Your head will then be held erect and safe.

9. When dry the surface is now sufficiently " dressed " to take colour.

I have found, however, that it pays handsomely to give the modelled head a thin coat of Wallart first before colouring. Wallart is a powder mixed with water which resembles somewhat the common plaster of paris. At one time I used plaster of paris, but found its brittle nature a decided drawback, so now I use Wallart, which

FIG. 18.

is tougher and incidentally gives a better surface for colouring.

When colouring the face avoid as far as possible any medium that will give a glossy surface. A high gloss catches the light and whereas it may be an advantage for your puppet's face to have a shiny nose, you do not necessarily want to produce an illuminated beacon. So use matt colours. Opaque colours of the poster, showcard

and powder colour variety.   All these colours dry with a
matt surface and so do not function as surface mirrors
and detract from the character.

You will notice that I have presupposed that you will
not necessarily want *hair* upon the head of this puppet.
Its hat may preclude such an addition.   But if you *do*
want hair upon the head of your character you can :

(*a*) Model it in the adhesive tissue paper, frilling the
paper to the style required ; *or*

(*b*) You can use crêpe hair or wool and build the hair
layer by layer to the required shape and fashion.

In sticking this hair into place use seccotine, for this I
have found to be the more suitable.

A glove puppet must have *hands*.

These should be carved from soft wood or modelled in
paper pulp according to the desire or capabilities of the
puppeteer.   The carved wooden hands are best since
these have *weight* and weight is useful in puppet work.
But too much weight is an undesirable nuisance like a
woman's superfluous fat. . . .

(*Fig.* 17 and *Fig.* 18).

CHAPTER SIX

CASTING A PUPPET HEAD

WHEN a collection of heads are required for a puppet play, some puppeteers prefer to make a number of a standard design. These standards then form the common base for all heads and all characteristics ; for example, different shaped noses, large or small, or caricatures of ears, smooth foreheads and overhanging brows, protruding chins or receding chins can then be added afterwards.

Oftentimes this is a device to be adopted with advantage, for you may be rushed for time. Also you may prefer to work from a standard model. It all depends upon yourself and the method you employ to achieve the best results.

Let us suppose therefore that you wish to standardise the head design, leaving peculiarities of feature to be added later. How shall we begin ?

First we model a head out of clay. For this you can use the grey clay of the sculptor which is remarkably cheap. Or you can use plasticene or glitter wax. You can use any plastic material that has a clay base.

When the head has been modelled to your satisfaction cut it down in half so that you separate the face from the back of the head.

Now make two plaster of paris moulds, one for the face and one for the back of the head.

When the plaster of paris sets, and it sets rapidly—too rapidly at times for the average user and the trouble begins—you possess two moulds ready for use.

Now take your tubes of plastic wood or your Barbola paste and press the selected medium well and truly *into* the plaster of paris mould. See that the medium is pressed *evenly* into the mould or you will find a face with the nose missing and that does not look so well. Press the plastic medium into the face mould and into the back of the head mould.

Leave for a while to dry slightly and then lift out. If you have difficulty in lifting out tap out carefully, tapping gently on the base of the mould.

Some folk find that a thin coat of oil, olive oil or linseed oil, brushed into the moulds first before impressing the parts facilitates the loosening. I think that you will be well advised to adopt this plan. It does help and it saves both time and trouble later.

When you have removed the front and the back of the head from the moulds—remember the plastic material is not yet fully dry, so be extra careful in the removal— clamp both part together to make a complete head. To be assured of a perfect fixing put a very thin layer of the plastic medium between each part and then close up. Press gently together and fill in the crack all round the head with the same plastic material to give a perfect finish.

I know of one puppeteer who prefers to wait until each half is fully dry before he joins up the parts. He works in plastic wood and joins up in plastic wood slightly touched with seccotine.

You will find out by experiment exactly which you prefer. The method you prefer will naturally be the one that gives you the best results in the shortest time. Yet although you will learn to work rapidly and accurately, remember this—rushing a job in puppetry never pays. Give yourself time. When I suggest you learn how to save time I am thinking in terms of an economy of time, not in terms of some slap-dash method. " That'll do " will get you nowhere in puppetry except in a most hopeless mess and I take it you do not wish the heads of your puppets to fall apart during a performance. It certainly will add humour to your production but not the humour you look for.

So save time by all means but do not sacrifice the craft for the sake of those few saved minutes. Those minutes are not saved. They are wasted !

CHAPTER SEVEN

SCENERY AND DESIGN

IN *Stage One* I gave you a brief survey of theatrical design. I did so advisedly for I want to impress upon you that except for a difference in *scale*, there is little that differs fundamentally between the model stage which you can erect in your own home, and the " legitimate " stage of the theatre proper.

Scale is the important factor and because of this I would suggest that you plan your production and your sets upon squared paper. Basically you have two sides, a rear " wall " and a floor to attend to. Without going into the eternal argument as to whether you should adopt the Fourth Wall Principle in production or not let me make my position quite clear.

When I produce a puppet play I pretend the whole time to *ignore* the audience. That is of a secondary consideration. The production of the *play* is the one thing that matters. So if your puppet turns his back upon the audience as he is speaking, so well and good. The only criterion to work upon is this. Would a human being, now being personated by a puppet, act so, speak so in ordinary everyday life ? If he would—go right ahead. If he would not—then make the puppet perform accurately in terms of human conduct.

So when you are designing a stage set for puppet plays, and when you are producing flesh and blood actors upon a large stage, ignore the audience. Take up your stand that the audience is looking into a room, listening in to the players, and the players do not know that there are eavesdroppers present. In parenthesis I would add that I would make it *compulsory* for everyone who intends to take up puppetry seriously to produce *at least once a year* a proper stage play upon a large stage, with human actors before a human audience. This can quite easily be done among puppet groups, if the will to do so is to be found there. Stage production upon a large scale is invaluable in puppet production. So too is stage designing.

Moreover, such a training would rid the puppet world of much of its superiority complex. There is no room in the world of art for snobs. Art is a gift given to man to be shared among men. It is not for the *coterie*. Pool your knowledge. Pool your experience. Throw everything you possess into the community kitty. Your puppet-lore belongs to the tribe. It is not a precious secret to be guarded by one selfish individual.

So treat the stage, your stage, you little theatre, as a small-scale version of the large stage. Square the whole thing up. For this I suggest you have at hand pieces of black cardboard.

Piece One represents the backcloth as seen by the audience, *after the wings have been removed.* Piece One, therefore, represents the whole surface area of the back-cloth as seen by the audience at the moment of maximum exposure.

Pieces Two and Three represent the side walls of the stage as seen by the audience. These pieces are whole. No doors, no windows, no gaps of any kind to be shown in them. They represent blank walls.

Piece Four represents the floor space as seen by the audience at the moment of maximum exposure.

All these pieces are of black cardboard. Upon that blackboard measure out and mark in, using Chinese white drawing ink, one-inch squares. This gives you a surface survey of the total areas available for decoration—in the case of the backcloth and the walls, and for position and placement of the properties and players in the case of the floor. You therefore leave nothing to hazard. When we are producing upon a big stage with human actors we are extremely careful that the action is unchecked by ill-placed properties. How much more reason there must be for us to see that the diminutive stage is kept free of annoying *impedimenta*, especially when you realise that it is an easy thing for a human to walk around an offending property, even to remove it casually as part of the " business " of the play, while the poor ham-strung puppet merely fouls his life-lines and in all probability collapses at the wrong moment !

So square up your stage area first, using white lines upon black cardboard. For this blackboard use a matt surface poster board. These are easily obtainable from any artists' colourman and they are cheap. Even if they cost ten times the few pence they do cost, they would be cheap at the price. They save a wastage of nervous energy and a deal of redrawing and replanning.

Once you have the sectionised base you can plot your stage. Where do you want the window ? Where the door ? How big will you require the window and the door ?

Where will you place your wings ? How far on to the stage will the wings project ? The play demands the use of a table, where is that table to be placed ? How much space will it take ? How much will the placing of the table affect the free passage of the puppets ?

When planning your set, lay sheets of thin white tracing paper over the sectionised boards. Sketch in the placements and position of properties and puppets. Use a " B " pencil for this. Then rough out your colour-scheme using crayons. Aim not so much at a finished drawing but at a swift impression.

Keep the stage as free as you can of properties. I remember a production I once saw of *The House With*

Twisty Windows. The stage was littered with boxes, a broken table, broken chairs and a divan, and *across* the room ran a clothes-line filled with nondescript washing. When I asked the producer why, he said he wanted to show the awful cramped condition under which this particular set of people were living. He certainly did that. No actor dare sit on a chair for fear it collapsed, and every time a character crossed the stage it got entangled either with the washing or in the clothes line. The whole production was absurd, spoiled by a lack of imagination. Avoid that over-stressing. Whatever you may feel privately about the intelligence of your particular audien ce, remember it pays, and pays handsomely, to treat them as if they really did possess intelligence. The audience will always respond.

Then there is the problem of *colour.* Here I am confronted by a tremendous difficulty. I find it practically impossible to give any hard and fast rules about colouring a stage set. Obviously it must depend upon the play you wish to produce, and the method and mode you mean to employ in the presentation. For example, you may wish to design your play in an austere fashion, as we saw several years ago in the *black and white* production of *Twelfth Night.* A bold experiment and to my mind a very successful one. Or you may wish to emulate the Chauve Souris and make of colour one of the actors upon the stage. Good again, but I think that you will see from both the examples I give here that the colour has been *controlled* and the controller is the stage designer, working in perfect harmony with the producer. If you are both designer and producer the problem solves itself, or should do. If, however, you are the designer, and you are working with a producer, or vice versa, then you two people must work *as one mind.* If you have an uncontrolled artistic temperament and want to work out your own design willy-nilly and ignore the suggestions of the producer, then were I the producer, I should throw you neck-and-crop out of the theatre, and there would be no may-be about that. The producer is the harmoniser. He must weld together scenery, players, lighting and music. It is in his hands to create a harmony or a discord. The conscientious producer will not allow of the discord. If he is obstructed, he should resign at once. The company can then stew in its own juice.

You see, once again I read the lesson of the stage to the amateur puppeteer. The theatre is the song of the arts, sung in harmony by all the devotees. It is either this— or nothing.

In colour you must subordinate your schemes to the spirit and to the interpretation of the play. It may mean that you may play upon the psychological influences of colour and make the key-board of the stage suggest the chords desired by the producer. In no case should the colour scheme overshadow or dwarf the action. The set must serve to enhance the spirit of the play. If the play is of the spirit beautiful, then let the scene be of the quiet beauty of early morn or of twilight. If the spirit of the play is harsh and cruel, design your set to show to better advantage the movement and motion of the production.

Remember, too, that you must consider the problem of lighting. Light, especially artificial light, plays havoc with colour. I was lecturing upon " Colour Theory " in a place where a blizzard had crashed a tree across the power station. All electricity failed. I lectured by candle-light. A quaint and withal a weird experience. Suddenly I stopped, all my colour charts were *wrong*. The candle-light had wrecked them, my blues had turned to black !

Do not be over-ambitious in your lighting systems. Keep to plain lights wherever possible and if you do want to introduce colour in your lighting do so sparingly—and decently. You are not a stunt electrician, and if you have a stunt electrician in your company keep him chained up until wanted and then let him loose only upon a lead. The temptation for a keen electrician to play whoopee in a model theatre is almost beyond human power to resist. You *must* resist him or he will destroy all with his dancing lights, his dimmers and his dynamo idiosyncrasies.

To return to colour again : use opaque colours as far as possible, and use the standard hues of the Ostwald circle. These are eight in number : Yellow, orange, red, purple, blue, turquoise, sea-green and leaf-green. To produce

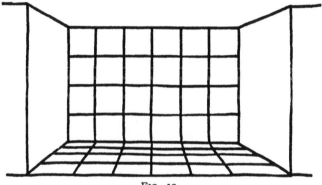

FIG. 19.

what we call the " broken colours," that is the tone values of the hues (the full colours), you may add white, grey or black in turn to the standard hues. By doing so you can produce a wide range of colours—by mixture.

Thus you may add *white* (*a*) to the eight standards and produce the *tints*. These are sometimes termed, and quite erroneously, the pastel shades. They are the soft colours that blend so delicately in costume as well as in scenery. You use the tints for distant scenery.

If you add *grey* (*g*) to the eight standards you produce what are known as the *shaded tints*, that is the grey colours. These are deeper in tone value and may be used for the middle distance in scenery painting.

If you add *black* (*n*) to the eight standards you produce the *shades.* The deep-toned colours so valuable for the foreground in scenery painting.

This leaves, if you wish it, the full hues for your costume.

Scenery and design may become effective only under control. Control of space, control of line, control of colour, and the man *in control* is the producer. He is the conductor of the orchestra of the arts. (*Fig.* 19).

CHAPTER EIGHT

TYPES OF THEATRES

THERE is a general opinion that model theatres comprise only two types: the marionette theatre, wherein the stringed puppets play; and the Punch and Judy show type, where one finds the glove puppets.

While it is readily admitted that these are the main types, there are others and it is of these other types I wish to write about now.

The marionette theatre I shall not refer to here, for I deal fully with it in *Stage Three*.

The Punch and Judy Show is familiar to all. It is a frame of wood, covered with a cloth " dress." (*Fig.* 20.)

Now for some at least of the others. I say " some " advisedly, for there are types a-plenty, but in the main they are the offshoots of certain basic types. It is the basic shapes I wish to deal with more specifically.

First, there is what is know as the *Still Theatre*. Here we find a box shape, with one side cut out to resemble a proscenium arch.

Inside this theatre the student of the drama sets up the scene·

FIG. 20.

Framework of Punch and Judy Show. Shaded parts represent wooden flats. All else in skeleton to take cloth covering.

of the play, cuts out the characters, and places them in position. The *Still Theatre* is therefore a spectacle. It records a special stage design, a special grouping of the characters. It is useful for story telling or for play readings. It creates an atmosphere. One often finds the *Still Theatre* erected in the greenroom of a theatre—nearly always in a Repertory Theatre, where a particularly beautiful design has been created.

So the *Still* is for recording. It is not for action. It is lighted as simply as possible. It can be made out of a cardboard box and is invaluable for experimental design. (*Fig. 21*).

Then there is the *Box Theatre*, which seems to have grown out of the *Still*. It is built in the same way, i.e., invariably it is a box. The lid of the box forms the " ceiling " of the stage. The front is open for the proscenium

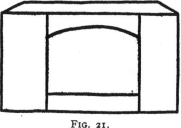

FIG. 21.
Still theatre.

arch. The sides are cut to represent the wings and this is used for elementary experiments, not only in design, but in action also. This type of model theatre is for the cut-out figures introduced on to the stage from the wings. (*Fig. 22.*)

Next we come to the *Panoramic Theatre*—a theatre again for cut-outs, " playing " before a moving background. This is an attractive device for children and helps to create the illusion of the figures walking from place to place without actually leaving the stage. By designing cut-out scenery, which is placed just in front of the panorama, the panoramic roll can represent the sky. So as the action goes forward in the country, the clouds go scudding across the sky. (*Fig* 23.)

The *Shadow Show*, another form of theatre, can be performed by cut-outs pushed upon the stage from the wings, or by puppets mounted upon long vertical rods and operated from beneath the stage.

These are basic types.   As I said above, there are others, but in the main these others are derivative.

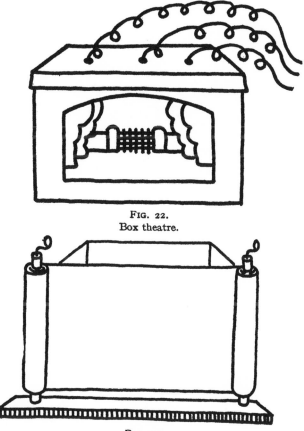

FIG. 22.
Box theatre.

FIG. 23.
Panoramic theatre seen from behind.   " A " is frame of theatre facing audience.

ECCE SIGNUM!

A Religio-Æsthetic Phantasy

By

ARTHUR B. ALLEN

Characters : CHARWOMAN
ARTIST (MR. VENABLES)
MR. POSTLETHWAITE
LADY DIANA EBERLIE
MR. VACHELL
MISS TENNANT
MISS SANDERSON
MR. FAY
PHŒBE

SETTING : *A Studio. A large canvas hangs upon the
centre of the rear wall and is draped with a curtain so
hung that it will drop at the right moment and leave the
picture exposed to the view.*
*Light falls directly upon it, and the room is flooded with
light coming from the left of the stage. The* CHARWOMAN
stands centre, resting upon her broom.

CHARWOMAN : Well, that's that. An' thank Gawd for it !
Makes a lot o' work these howdydo shows. *Private
Shows* the papers call 'em. Can't see the use of 'em
meself. If you paints a pitcher says I—show it.
Don't keep it 'ere like this, all wrapped up like a sore
finger. Goin' to be 'zibited 'e says. Goin' to 'ave a
lot-a swells comin' to see it. Them as knows wot's
wot. Yeah. I knows the sort they are.
Better be goin', I s'pose. Late now. Funny
bein' 'ere now everythin's cleared away. Don't
look right. Too clean an' tidy.
That's a funny pitcher that is, hid up be'ind that
bit o'curtain. It ain't a natur' pitcher 'e says. It's
got a tree in it, anyway, an' you can see it is a tree.
That's sumthin'. 'E says it was a—a—wot did 'e

say now ?—a metta-bia-fustical con-volushun. Yes,
that's it. Wot the 'ell that is I *don't* know.
Put some writin' under it 'e 'as. Did it yesterd'y.
Esse sig-um. Funny langwidge. But it's sumthin' to
'ave some writin' under it. Wot 'appens most times,
you gets writin' you can understand and a pitcher
you can't. But 'e's got a pitcher that looks like a
pitcher in some ways, an' now I can't read wot's
wrote. It's all bung-eye to me. Ain't got a culter'd
min', that's wot it is. 'E was right w'en 'e says that
to me. O' lor', 'ere 'e comes, an' I ain't gorn.

ARTIST (*off*) : You there, Mrs. Horribin ?

CHARWOMAN : Yessir. I'm jest finished an' I'm jest
goin'.

ARTIST (*off*) : Good. Come here before you go, will you ?

CHARWOMAN : Yessir. That's me money 'e's goin' to give
me. That's all right then. I works for dough and
'e paints for dough, both of us 'ave got to 'ave dough,
even if 'e is cultured. Better go an' get it I s'pose.
'Is money's all right, even if 'is painting ain't.
(*Exit.*)

ARTIST (*off*) : There you are, Mrs. Horribin, you'll find
that's right, I think.

CHARWOMAN (*off*) : Thank *you*, sir. Yessir, that's right,
sir. Goo' afternoon, sir.

ARTIST (*off*) : Good afternoon. You'll be here in the
morning ?

CHARWOMAN (*off*) : Yessir. I'll be 'ere. They'll 'ave
made a tidy mess o' the place, I warrant. Good-day,
sir. (*The* CHARWOMAN *may be heard retreating,
humming as she goes. The* ARTIST *enters studio,
right*).

ARTIST : Quite a character that woman. All's ready
now. Ah ! The pot of daffodils will look very well
placed here. I'll fetch it. (*Goes off, right, and returns*

*immediately with pot of daffodils upon a tall table.
This he places in the centre of the stage, by the side of the
picture.*)

That's better. Looks more art-y now. (*Ha-ha!*)
Art-y. Bah! An ugly word! Full of hypocrisy!
But that's what they come here for. For—for art.
Then they'll ask me how could I think out my
thoughts and put them on canvas. And do I sit, and
sit, and sit, until inspiration drives me to the paint
and I paint as if possessed of a demon. Good
Lord! They little know that inspiration does not
come until a hell of a lot of work has been done.
Trial and error and all that. Mustn't tell 'em that
though. Too commercial for these soul slaverers.
So I talk tosh about headaches and inspiration,
æsthetics and aspirin, artless art and spiritual
uplift. Hell! It's enough to make a man vomit.

Time's getting along I see. They're due here any
minute. Mrs. Horribin was late in going to-day.
Would tidy the place up. My God! and I should
think she has. I'll never be able to find a damn
thing. Oh, well, if this goes well I shall be able to
go into retreat for a bit, then it will seem a great
adventure to come back here and find things again.

It's up to you, old picture. You've got to work
the oracle for me. You're a funny devil, but you're
ambitious, and I'm proud of you. You're strong in
line and simple. Too simple for these folks, I expect.
They want cubes and prisms and truncated cones.
You'll disappoint some of them I don't doubt. But,
never mind, Ecce, old man. You'll do, and if you
don't, well damn 'em and that's all there is in that.
(*Door bell rings.*) Here's the first. Old Postlethwaite, I'll bet my boots. (*Voices.*) Yes, it is.
(*Enter* MR. POSTLETHWAITE.) Good afternoon, Mr.
Postlethwaite. You are the first as always.

MR. POSTLETHWAITE : 'Afternoon, Mr. Venables. Gad !
Those stairs, those stairs ! They break my wind
every time I climb them. Why can't you paint on
the ground floor ? Not enough light you will say.
I know. I know. I know every word you artists
say as well as if I said it myself. Ah, well ! And now
what have you to show me this time ?

ARTIST : Yes, we have to work in the attic, for light as
you say.

MR. POSTLETHWAITE : As I said. Now what is it this
time ?

ARTIST : It's a painting as usual. But a little unusual,
I hope.

MR. POSTLETHWAITE : Unusual ? Good, I'm tired of all
these things you artists hackney. I've just come
from the Italian Exhibition. Well, well. I never
was so bored in all my life. Madonnas, Madonnas,
Madonnas and The Child. Millions of them, everywhere, and where there were no Madonnas there were
people. What the devil so many people could see in
an art show I don't know. My feet were crushed, sir,
crushed and by people in an art show. Most of 'em
women, damn 'em. I hate all women when I find
'em in any sort of an exhibition. These shows are
for men, men of taste and distinction, not for women.

ARTIST : I have not been to that show. I shall not go
either.

MR. POSTLETHWAITE : Not go, Mr. Venables ? But it is
your duty to go.

ARTIST : Then I shall fail in my duty. I've seen many
of the pictures, but I've seen them quietly, alone
with them and my thoughts. They have inspired
some of my greatest thoughts, and I'll not prostitute
those memories for the sake of a queue and crushed
toes, not even for you, Mr. Postlethwaite, much as I
value your opinion.

MR. POSTLETHWAITE : Of course not, of course not. I quite understand. I appreciate the artist, his quietude and his inspiration. I often feel that if I had quiet moments I, too, might—you know—create. (*Ring on bell interrupts him.*)

ARTIST : Excuse me, Mr. Postlethwaite, I'll see who this is. (*Exit, right.*)

MR. POSTLETHWAITE : Venables always gets a lot of folk to see his shows, folk who know nothing, abso-bally-lutely nothing about art. Folk who don't know the difference between a Botticelli and an Epstein. Wonder what he's got under that rag ? No, I won't. I'll wait until he lets me see. Gives me a thrill. The curtain falls, and behold, the picture. That reminds me, what's he calling this one ? *Ecce Signum !* "Behold the sign !" That's what Falstaff said. Funny. What's this fellow doing with Falstaff ?

All artists are the same, mad, but it's good to know them. They are as contradictory as doctors. Anyway, I collect artists. (*Voices coming nearer.*) Who's this ? (*Enter* ARTIST, MISS TENNANT, MISS SANDERSON, MR. VACHELL *and* LADY DIANA EBERLIE).

ARTIST : There is no need for me to introduce you all. You have met before.

LADY DI : How do you do, Mr. Postlethwaite ? I knew you would be here first. I said so to Vach-y, didn't I ?

MR. VACHELL : That's right. You always are, you know. How do, Postlethwaite ?

MR. POSTLETHWAITE : Good to see all you folk again. Knew you were coming. And how are you, Miss Tennant ?

MISS TENNANT : Very busy at the moment. I have hurried away from a new work, so fascinating.

MR. VACHELL : Yes. Miss Tennant has just started a clinic for the psychological analysis of the children of confirmed drunkards, and she is finding her time fully occupied.

MR. POSTLETHWAITE : Now that is very interesting, and what have you found out up to now, Miss Tennant ?

MISS TENNANT : I must confess, nothing. You see we have only just fixed up the position of the clinic, and I have been there all the morning attending to the furnishing and so forth. I want a play-room for the children where they can be watched under expert control. Oh, there are so many things to be considered, you know.

ARTIST : I am sure your work will meet with the success it deserves, Miss Tennant.

MISS TENNANT : That is so nice of you, Mr. Venables, so kind.

ARTIST : And you, Miss Sanderson, have you been busy, too ?

MISS SANDERSON : Yes, very so. I am now trying to illustrate Omar Khayyam in wood blocks, and I find it terribly difficult.

ARTIST : Beyond all doubt. The Eastern atmosphere is almost beyond our artists, unless they have Eastern blood in their veins. Unless also there are signs of genius, and according to the newspapers, your last show was very well received.

MR. POSTLETHWAITE : It was, Venables, it was. I was able to sell about two-thirds of the exhibits for Miss Sanderson. (*The bell rings again.*)

ARTIST : That is Fay, the poet, I expect. He is the last visitor I am expecting.

LADY DI : Only such a few of us this time, Mr. Venables. Why is that ?

ARTIST : This is a peculiar picture and I wanted to choose my visitors with tremendous care. Excuse me, I will meet him as he comes in. He is a shy man. (*Exit.*)

LADY DI : Very nicely put, but I would not have worn

this gown had I known it was to be a cabal and not a gathering.

ARTIST : Come inside, Mr. Fay. Allow me to introduce you. Ladies and Gentlemen, Mr. Fay, the poet. Lady Diana Eberlie, famed for her hospitality and, pardon an artist's privilege, famed for her beauty also. Miss Sanderson, whose illustrations I know you admire. Miss Tennant, an untiring social worker among our less fortunate fellows. Mr. Vachell, a connoisseur, and Mr. Postlethwaite, who has done so much for rising artists both here and in America. It was Mr. Postlethwaite who was responsible for the Cubist Exhibition from America. (*As* MR. FAY *goes round he murmurs greeting and then turns to* MR. VENABLES.)

MR. FAY : I have taken a great liberty, Mr. Venables.

ARTIST : Oh ?

MR. FAY : I have brought along my little girl. She is downstairs. I would like her to see your pictures. She is only a kid, but very interested in pictures. And she *would* come.

LADY DI : How exquisite. Let me plead for her, Mr. Venables.

ARTIST : The daughter of Mr. Fay is very welcome, but had I had any doubts you would have dispelled them, Lady Diana.

LADY DI (*laughs*) : Flatterer !

MR. FAY : Then I will call her up. Thank you. (*His voice may be heard off as he goes out to call.*) Phœbe !

PHŒBE (*off*) : Yes, Daddy ?

MR. FAY : Come upstairs. (*Steps approach and then* MR. FAY *returns with his daughter, a girl of some ten years of age.*)

ARTIST : How do you do, Phœbe ? This is a great treat for me.

PHŒBE : I told Daddy you wouldn't mind. You don't, do you ?

ARTIST : I love having you. Now we are all met I will drop the curtain. But a word before I do so. I have taken a very peculiar subject, and it has been difficult. For months it would not come. The canvas was bare and stayed bare. Then in a flash it came, and I have fixed the vision on the canvas. They say a picture is the child of the painter. If that is so, and I believe it must be so, then this is my dearest child, my perfect child.

LADY DI : How beautifully expressed.

ARTIST : I have christened my child *Ecce Signum !* Or as friend Falstaff would have said : " Behold the sign." It is a sign I have painted. This is the sign.

(He pulls a cord and the curtain falls, revealing a large figure of a man-shape. All in lines, and in the well of two lines where arms would have appeared in a realistic picture stands a pine tree.)

It is my idea of God.

(They cluster around the canvas which dominates the group. MR. POSTLETHWAITE soon extricates himself.)

MR. POSTLETHWAITE : Well, I'm . . . I always said all the damned artists were mad, but this is the maddest of the lot.

(MR. FAY and his little daughter are on the fringe of the group. MR. FAY is impressed, he has caught the feeling of the picture and sees in it not a decoration but a philosophy akin to his own.)

MR. FAY : This is your best work, Venables. It will help you considerably. But your idea is wide and will be misunderstood.

ARTIST : Thank you, Mr. Fay. I fully expect it will raise a storm.

PHŒBE : What did he say it was, Daddy ?

MR. FAY : It is a picture of God, dear.

PHŒBE : It isn't, Daddy.

ARTIST : Ah ! And what do you think it is, Phœbe ?

PHŒBE : I don't know. I've never seen a picture like that before.

MISS TENNANT : She is too young yet to understand God.

PHŒBE : I'll show you God. (*Goes to the table where the daffodils stand, and takes a bloom.*) Here is God.

MR. FAY : Phœbe. Come here, child. I am sorry, Venables.

ARTIST : Splendid ! Nothing to be sorry about, Fay. I'm afraid I agree.

LADY DI : What an original child. (*And the company stand and look at* PHŒBE *as the curtain falls.*)

PUPPETRY FOR BEGINNERS

STAGE THREE

CHAPTER ONE

HOW TO BEGIN

FIRST things first.

Which comes first ?

The puppet or the play ?

In this I assume you are making your puppets for the first time, that you have never done puppetry before, that you wish to begin—now.

That was why I began with the assertion of *First things first*.

The first thing to be considered in puppetry is the play. First and last and all the time your mind should be centred upon the play and upon its development, its presentation and interpretation.

You say to yourself : " I'm going to produce this play because I want to produce this play, because I believe I know just how to interpret it. I shall use puppets for my company of actors."

You do not say : " I possess a lovely set of marvellous dolls. What can I produce that will show off their beauty ?"

So if you wish to become a real puppeteer you must be a reader of plays and a producer of plays, who uses puppets as a means to an end.

Having got that, I hope, quite clear, let us turn to the puppets themselves.

A word of warning here.

Ambition is a fine quality in a man, but too much ambition in the early days of puppetry may lead to heart-break. Puppets possess temperament. They are human, although it may strike you as a little strange to read this before you have tried your luck. But when you *have* tried, you will the more fully appreciate what I mean.

Begin carefully.

Begin well.

Begin with *one* puppet, and find a one-puppet play.

If you are an adult who is reading this, read *Before Breakfast* by Eugene O'Neill. If you like it—produce it. It allows for a one-puppet interpretation.

Or you may like to produce *Nemo*. You will find that in *Stage One*.

If you are young and just beginning puppetry, you might like to make a little play for yourself of Scrooge sitting talking to himself, crouched over his tiny spark of a fire in his room just before Marley's Ghost appears.

If you want to go farther you could introduce Marley's Ghost as a beam of light, or as a *cut-out*, and so have one working puppet and one still figure.

Or you might make a puppet representing Old Æsop, telling one of his fables to the audience.

Old or young, whoever you are, if you are a beginner, begin easily and steadily with a one-puppet play. This will give you an opportunity to get used to the manipulation of the jointed figure, and having only one you can concentrate upon that one until you feel you begin to understand its idiosyncrasies and its moods, until you feel you have mastered the little joker. . . .

Then to begin you must experiment, and this time choose a play which will enable you to present two puppets. Here, of course, you have a much wider choice, and so here are a few suggestions for you :

1. A puppet interpretation of *La Belle Dame sans Merci* (Keats). The picture presents a knight asleep being visited in his dream by " a fairy child."

2. A puppet interpretation of the ballad *Sing Me a Song O*, from Gilbert and Sullivan.

3. *Scrooge and Marley*—both jointed puppets now.

4. *Where Are You Going To, My Pretty Maid ?*

5. *Knock, Knock, Knock*. The Porter Scene from *Macbeth*.

6. *Launcelot and Old Gobbo*, from *The Merchant of Venice*.

7. *Father Keegan and The Grasshopper*. Scene from *John Bull's Other Island*.

8. Prologue to *Androcles and The Lion* (G. B. Shaw).

From two-puppet plays you might like to try the combination of puppet with cut-outs. Then you could give Mark Antony's speech, his funeral oration to Cæsar.

From this point onwards you will have a clear field. Favourites among puppeteers are *Lima Beans, The Little Plays of St. Francis, The Man With a Flower in His Mouth*, and *Aria da Capo*.

I have not yet seen, and I would like to see, *The Apple Tree*, by Harold Chapin, interpreted as a puppet play. I believe puppets would do the work exceedingly well.

To be a successful puppeteer you must be a play-reader. You *must* be a play-reader even if you cannot write your own plays.

But try to write your own plays. Start off with the idea that you want to tell a story.

1. Write the story down in colloquial English as if you were telling it to your bosom friend, by your own fireside on a winter night, with the logs burning and a frost on the window panes outside. Make it intimate. Just " talk " naturally as you write that story.

2. Now read over the story. Make a list of the

characters in the story. What does each character say.
Write this down in dialogue form thus :

MAN : Where have you been ?
. BOY : Nowhere.
MAN : Where have you come from ?
BOY : Nowhere.
MAN : Then what are you doing ?
BOY : Nothing. I'm going home.

Plan the dialogue in short, snappy, pithy sentences.
Make them tell the tale without the waste of a word.
Remember that scene in *The Merchant of Venice* where
Bassanio is sounding Shylock for a loan ?

SHYLOCK : Three thousand ducats ; well.
BASSANIO : Ay, sir, for three months.
SHYLOCK : For three months ; well.
BASSANIO : For the which, as I told you, Antonio shall
    be bound.
SHYLOCK : Antonio shall become bound ; well.
BASSANIO : May you stead me ?   Will you pleasure me ?
    Shall I know your answer ?
SHYLOCK : Three thousand ducats for three months,
    and Antonio bound.
BASSANIO : Your answer to that.
SHYLOCK : Antonio is a good man.
BASSANIO : Have you heard any imputation to the
    contrary ?
SHYLOCK : Ho, no, no, no, no ; my meaning, in saying he
    is a good man, is to have you understand me, that he
    is sufficient. Yet his means are in supposition :
    he hath an argosy bound to Tripolis, another to the
    Indies ; I understand, moreover, upon the Rialto,
    he hath a third at Mexico, a fourth for England, and
    other ventures he hath, squandered abroad ; but
    ships are but boards, sailors but men : there be
    land-rats and water-rats, water thieves and land

thieves, I mean pirates ; and then there is the peril
of waters, winds and rocks. The man is, notwith-
standing, sufficient. Three thousand ducats ; I
think I may take his bond.

BASSANIO : Be assured you may.

SHYLOCK : I will be assured I may ; and, that I may be
assured, I will bethink me. May I speak with
Antonio ?

BASSANIO : If it pleases you to dine with us.

SHYLOCK : Yes, to small pork ; to eat of the habitation
which your prophet the Nazarite conjured the devil
into. I will buy with you, sell with you, talk with
you, walk with you, and so following ; but I will
not eat with you, drink with you nor pray with you.
What news on the Rialto ? Who is he comes here ?

There you have the whole story in a nutshell. It
begins with no unnecessary preliminaries. It rushes on,
laying bare all the factors upon which the play must
subsequently devolve.

Let us now suppose that you had chosen your play,
that you are determined to produce the play. Good.
We can now get to work and make the puppet.

CHAPTER TWO

THE POINTS OF A PUPPET

You know as well as I do that a dog entered as a competitor in a dog show is adjudicated by an assessment of its " points." The winning dog is the animal which runs true to type, or which is, in the opinion of the judges, the nearest to the accepted standard of a perfect type.

Puppets have their points also. But there is a deal more latitude in the points of the perfect puppet than is allowable in the points of the perfect dog.

What *is* a perfect puppet ?

This is an important question, for the puppet may be point device perfect and yet be a *bad* puppet.

Yes. A puppet may be beautifully made, a veritable work of art and still be a bad puppet ? Why ? It may be a puppet that just will not work.

What you must aim at is a puppet that will respond at once to the touch of the strings, a puppet which is nervously " alive " and responsive. It may be that your doll is out of proportion, is ugly, is stolid, is sour, yet when commanded it will obey. From my point of view I do not care how crude a puppet may be, how ugly, how stolid, but if it will act its part as and when required, that is the perfect puppet for me. And when all is said and done it is not the Adonis of the stage who makes the finest actor. Some of our greatest actors, yes and some of our greatest actresses, too, have little or no claim to personal beauty, either of face or even of proportions, yet they have become our brightest lights on the stage—because they are alive, and nervously aware of the vibrant chords of human emotions. It would be invidious for me to mention by name such men and women. It would be unfair. *They* would not mind, for they believe their art to transcend all other things in life, but their fan-mail might object very strongly and I have no desire to seek a premature grave !

Allowing for all this, which I may call the human element in the puppet, the fact still remains that we should try as far as it is possible and within our power to try, we should try to create a good puppet. Good— in so far as the puppet is a perfect puppet. Just as we strive through our various health and beauty exercises to produce a race of Venuses.

The points of a puppet therefore are *three* in number.

First.—You should aim to produce a puppet which corresponds to the proportions of a well-developed human body. Because the question of proportion is a vital one. I deal with it under a separate heading elsewhere (see *Proportions of the Human Body*).

The *first* point is to see that your puppet proportions are accurate.

Second.—Given your proportions to be accurate, aim at a lifelike interpretation of a character. Make your puppet *look alive*. Not only must the puppet *look alive*, it must also act as if it *were alive*, and this gives us our third point.

Third.—Aim to produce a series of natural movements. Sticking joints and jerky action may be all right in a farce or in a fantasy, they have no place in a human drama. A scene taken from *R.U.R.* in which the robots appear—this will allow of a harsh mechanical movement, yet even there it is wiser to rely upon the skilful manipulation of smooth-running joints than to be dependent upon a sticking joint. After all, even though the robots did move like slow-motion piston rods, there was a smooth rhythm even in that slow motion.

Aim therefore at flexibility and you cannot go wrong.
We have not finished yet.

Although the three main points of a good puppet are :

(1) good human resemblance :

(2) good proportions ;

(3) flexibility

—there are other supplementary points to be considered.

(*a*) The puppet undressed must look well. When dressed it must look perfect, as if it had been, as it were, poured into its costume.   In a word, see that the clothing of the puppet maintains an appreciation of *line*, as a well-dressed man always looks—as if he has been poured into his clothes.   It is a question more of a Bond Street tailor *versus* an off-the-peg clothier.   The one dresses his subject, the other subjects his customer to a dress.   The one produces an animated clothes-horse upon which he hangs in an indifferent manner any form of costume or suiting.

So—whether your puppet character be a courtier or a clown, a Piccadilly dude or a tramp—dress carefully and dress perfectly.   A badly dressed puppet can so easily destroy the stage illusion.   Even tramps, you know—stage tramps I mean, of course—conform to a type. There is artistry in their very raggedness.

Clothing the puppet is a point upon which great care must be expended.

(*b*) Then the puppet must be as perfectly balanced as it is possible to make it.   Humanity walks more or less in an upright position since the days of *Pithecanthropus erectus*.   And humanity walks more or less in an evenly balanced walk upon its two feet.   So see that feet and hands are weighted to keep the puppet upon the stage. Remember that unless you are modelling a hollow head the head is a weighty business.   If you do not counter-balance the head you will produce a variation of the

Quasimodo type, all head and spindly legs and inadequate feet.

Head and trunk are in the solid as a general rule. The legs weigh only a fraction of the combined mass of head *plus* trunk. If you give your puppet a detached pelvic girdle then you should weight that, too. I will deal with that later in this work.

(c) Finally there is the question of *control*. A puppet is not a mechanical clockwork figure which you wind up and let loose upon the stage. It is a double-jointed, epileptic, cataleptic figure, prone to collapse into an all-in wrestling throw position without a single word of provocation. . . . Its movements depend entirely upon you and you operate the puppet from above, by strings, attached to a control stick at one end and to certain points of the puppet at the other.

Remember what I have said already in this series—a puppet possesses temperament, it is wilful and wayward. It says : " Shan't " more often than it obeys—if you will allow it to. You must be the puppet's *master*. You maintain your mastery of the puppet through the control strings, as a careful father curbs his extravagant son through the tightening of his purse-strings.

You must be as careful in the arrangement, the organisation and the manipulation of the controls as you have been in achieving proportion and costume and line. Again, because of the importance of the controls I shall deal with this as a specific subject later in this book.

Having regimented the various and essential points of the puppet we can proceed to the creation of the puppet itself.

CHAPTER THREE

PUPPET heads may be constructed in several ways. They may be :

    (*a*) carved out of wood,

    (*b*) made from paper pulp and finished with a surface dressing, *or*

    (*c*) carved or cast in Wallart.

Let us take each of these three types in turn and see how we may fashion a puppet head accordingly.

(*a*) A PUPPET HEAD CARVED OUT OF WOOD.

You must select a type of wood that is not too soft. Soft wood certainly cuts easily, but it has an annoying tendency to tear as you carve and so spoil your work. Although the choice is not universally popular I carve my puppet heads from pitch-pine. Using keen tools you can achieve good clean work. Blunt tools are useless, anyway. But keep those tools sharp.

Take a leaf from the notebook of the woodcarver. He always keeps his tools " touched up " and he " touches up " after every two or three cuts. Keen tools are your greatest friends, blunted tools your worst enemies.

Birch is, I believe, the one wood more commonly used among serious puppeteers. It does not rip as you cut, for it has a close, tight grain.

The grain of the wood is important here, as it is important anywhere in wood-carving.

You must cut *away from* the grain.

Fig. 1 gives you the directions of the first cuts. Here you begin to shape the head in the rough.

Fig. 2 shows the next series of cuts required. The head becomes more symbolic in shape.

Fig. 3 gives you a rough idea of what the back view of *Fig.* 2 will look like. Remember that the area between

FIG. 1.

First cut. Cut away all the solid black parts.

points " A " and " B " really slope away from you from " A " to " B."

Fig. 4 shows the neck taking shape.

Fig. 5. More detail added to the head lines.

Fig. 6. The ears appear in the solid. No detail yet for the ears.

Fig. 7 recalls *Fig.* 2 to lead us into the projection shown in *Fig.* 8.

Fig. 8 shows the rough shape of the face from the front.

Fig. 9. A diagrammatic expression of the profile of your puppet.

Fig. 10 shows, in projections from *Fig.* 9, the dropping back of the planes of the face to throw in relief the ridge above the eyes and the nose.

FIG. 2.

Second cuts. Cut away on the solid black part.

Fig. 11 is symbolic and shows on the shaded area where the wood has been cut back to throw eye-ridge, nose and mouth into relief.

Fig. 12 follows hard upon the heels of *Fig.* 11 and shows the details added for eyes and mouth.

These are your main lines of direction. Your puppet has now a stark and strongly lined face. If you wish to

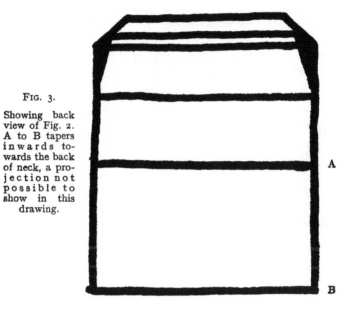

FIG. 3.

Showing back view of Fig. 2. A to B tapers inwards towards the back of neck, a projection not possible to show in this drawing.

A

B

FIG. 4.

Third cut. Beginning to shape the neck. (Back view.)

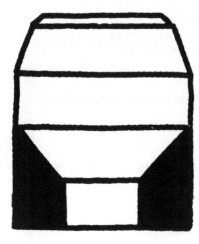

FIG. 5.

Fourth cut. Shaping the
head into the neck.
(Back view.)

FIG. 6.

Fifth cut,
indicating the
position of the
ears.
(Back view.)

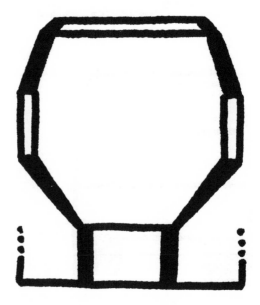

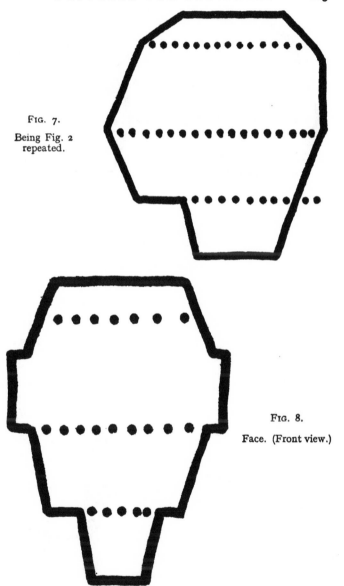

FIG. 7.

Being Fig. 2 repeated.

FIG. 8.

Face. (Front view.)

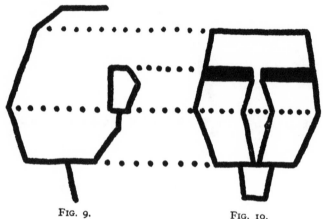

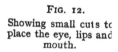

FIG. 9.

FIG. 10.
Cut back for ridge above eyes.

FIG. 12.
Showing small cuts to
place the eye, lips and
mouth.

FIG. 11.
Showing side view of Fig. 10. The
shaded portion cutting back to
throw up nose in relief.

introduce softer lines, rounded edges and generally a more naturalistic effect, smooth off the angles, using either a small rasp or sandpaper.

(*b*) PUPPET HEAD FROM PAPER PULP.

For this you require :

(*a*) a fairly thick dowel rod ;

(*b*) a piece of stout wood, into which you drill a hole so that you may insert the dowel rod and stand it upright.

FIG. 13.

This hole may, of course, be drilled into your carpenter's bench, or into your work-table, if you are fortunate enough to be working on either of these quite necessary surfaces. You can, of course, hold the dowel upright by clamping it into a vice. (*Fig.* 13.)

Around the dowel's end, after covering it with a liberal layer of glue, build up an egg shape in paper pulp. For the pulp use old newspaper, soaked overnight in clean water. Squeeze out the surplus water. Pulp the paper in a pestle and mortar, or in an earthernware jar—a honey jar serves admirably with a stump stick. Pound the paper to a pulp. Take out. Squeeze out once again any surplus water. Pour over the pulp an adhesive, such as L.A.P. water paste, or Gloy or even flour paste. If you use flour paste, add a little gold size. Do not make the pulp too wet. Keep it " tacky."

Using your hands, build the egg-shape around the dowel-end, pressing the pulp towards the central stave. (*Fig.* 14.)

Fig. 14.

When you judge you have the egg of sufficient size for the puppet you propose to make, leave to dry. It is, therefore, advisable for you to make several of these shapes at one and the same time. This will save you hours of labour later on.

When the core is dry, take tissue paper. Tear the tissue into narrow strips. Cover the strips with an adhesive, and bind around until the whole core is covered with tissue paper. Smooth all rough edges down by stroking the surface evenly with the thumb. (*Fig.* 15.)

Now take some *Barbola* paste and cover the core with this plastic medium. Cover thickly and press the

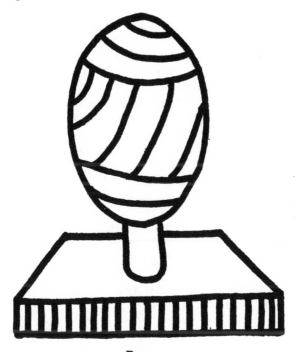

FIG. 15.

Barbola well on to the core. Again some folk feel that an adhesive is required to assure that the *Barbola* will remain in position. If you feel that way, too, then cover the core with *Newstick*. This is the perfect adhesive for use with *Barbola* paste. So let us do that.

Cover the core with *Newstick* first. Then lay on your *Barbola* paste, pressing the paste firmly on to the

K

foundation, *but*—have more *Barbola*, i.e., a thicker layer of *Barbola* all over the core than you will require.

Model this plastic medium into a roughly shaped head. You can do this with your fingers and thumbs. Once you have this rough shape indicated you can at once proceed to fashion in greater detail.

For the fashioning use a wooden modelling tool, such as you will find in a plasticene set.

Raise the ridge of the skull a little to allow for the eyebrows. Sink the medium back a little from the eyes. Model the nose. Mark clearly the planes of the cheeks. Bring out the lips, drop the underlip back slightly to the chin. Model a firm chin. Trim and slope gently down to the throat. (*Fig.* 16.)

If you wish to introduce character lines into your puppet face, now is the time to do so. Bring the eyes close together, to the bridge of the nose, for a shifty character. Set the eyes wide apart for an honest fellow. Square the jaw and jut out the chin for an aggressive type. Make a receding chin for the congenital idiot or the weakling.

Study faces. Study types. Look up types of noses, ears, eyes, mouths in a good encyclopædia. These are classified in terms of the portrayal of character. Use this information and humanise your puppet.

Smooth the surface with thumb and finger and the modelling tool. Aim for expression and avoid minute detail. Minute detail fogs the issue. Model boldly and to plan. Stick to your plan. Do not, whatever happens, change your mind in the middle of the modelling. If you do it will show.

To colour the head, use a good water-colour. You can use the *Barbola* colours if you prefer, but water-colours will serve your purpose.

You can use *Wallart* instead of *Barbola* if you prefer. If you do—then mix *Wallart* powder into a thick paste

and cover the core, using a small tapering palette knife.
Lay on thickly.   Leave to dry for a while.   *Wallart* takes
a long time to set, so that once the surface wetness has
evaporated you can pinch, and shape and model as you
did with *Barbola.*   Model as for *Barbola.*   You will find

Fɪɢ. 16.

that *Wallart* works much more coarsely than does *Barbola*
paste.   This is not a deterrent, for when dry you can cut
and carve a *Wallart* surface, using an ordinary penknife
and a " V " or a " U " lino-cutting gouge.

   As you have modelled the head you have shaped the
neck at the same time.   This is done almost automatically

for you naturally "pull down" on to the dowel, the plastic medium.

Using a sharp tenon saw, or alternatively, a sharp fine-bladed fretsaw, cut off the superfluous length of the dowel rod. This leaves you with the neck, in wood, all ready for the insertion of the screw-eye, by which you will attach the head to the body.

Insert that screw-eye very carefully or you will split the dowel rod. Use a cobbler's awl and make the first incision in the dowel before attempting to drive in the screw-eye.

You should keep a cobbler's awl always at hand. It is a valuable accessory in all puppet work.

Since the manipulation strings have to be affixed to the side of the head you must insert the fixing points. Some puppeteers prefer to place a wire *right through* the core before the outer covering is added (*Fig.* 17). They then bend each end into a tiny loop and model around each loop. I find this method a little tiresome. I prefer to make the head first and then when the head is nearly dry I drive in the tiniest screw-eyes obtainable. The setting medium helps cement the threads. Especially is this so if you dip the threads of the screw into *Newfix* first.

If you feel more confident with the wire going right through the head, bore through carefully with the cobbler's awl. Squeeze a little *Newfix* into each hole and then thread the wire very carefully through the head. Bend over the free ends and make the string loops.

The *position* of these head-points is important. They must be so placed that the head is held erect. If you place your points too far forward the head tilts backwards. If they are placed too far back the head tilts forward. The best place for the suspension points is just *above* the ears.

This gives a vertical hang to the head and this is what you require.   You see now that if you have a character in your play, like Scrooge, for example, who walks with his head bowed forward, then you can get that effect by the correct placing of the suspension points.   These points are of major importance.

For hair you may use either ordinary wool or tow, or crêpe hair.

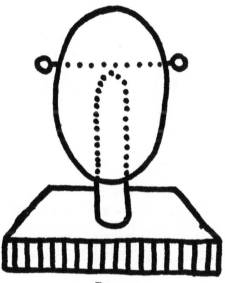

FIG. 17.

(c) PUPPET HEAD MADE FROM WALLART.

Wallart is a powder which when mixed with water makes a paste.   This paste can be cut and carved and it does not crumble, as does plaster of paris.   It is a superior medium to plaster of paris in all respects.

It is possible therefore to carve a puppet head out of *Wallart* in the solid.   But this way takes a long time to dry.

Suppose you wish to make a fairly large head. Then cut four pieces of cardboard, say three inches by four inches, so that when put together they make a four-sided box. Cut a piece of cardboard to act as a loose base. Set up the " box " and keep in position with three elastic bands. Leave the baseboard loose.

Mix the *Wallart* fairly thickly, i.e., do not have it watery. The wetter you have the *Wallart* the longer it takes to dry. That much is pretty obvious.

Pour the *Wallart* into the container, leave to dry. When the surface begins to set take the mass—but keep the cardboard sides in position—off the baseboard and place upon a perforated grid. You can use for this a fine wire mesh or a perforated zinc plate such as may still be found in old-fashioned soap dishes. If these are not procurable then make a grid yourself out of pieces of wire, knitting needles or narrow strips of wood and put the *Wallart* block upon the grid. The wire will allow the air to get underneath and will also allow any surplus water to drain off.

When nearly dry, remove the side boards, and allow to dry thoroughly. It is a good plan to cover the side boards with a thin coat of vaseline before pouring in the *Wallart*. You can prevent any possible sticking that way.

Once the block is dry, cut and carve as you would if you were carving wood.

If, however, you wish to standardise your puppet heads then model the head *first* in plasticene. Make a mould of the head, using plaster of paris. Remember that such a head must be in halves. The front of the head constitutes one mould, the back the second.

When the moulds are dry, give a coat of oil on the inside of the mould to prevent sticking. Mix up *Wallart* into a thick consistency, i.e., mix the powder with water until all the powder has gone—just gone. Drop the *Wallart* into the moulds. Spread out so that all crevices are filled.

Leave to dry. When *nearly* dry, carefully remove the two parts of the head. With *thin Wallart*, brush a coat over the flat sections. Put the back of the head and front of the head together and press gently together. Leave to dry.

When modelling in plasticene allow for the neck. When you clamp the halves together insert the screw-eye into the neck and leave to dry. If the division shows around the head fill up with *Wallart*.

Cut and carve any additional detail you may think necessary.

CHAPTER FOUR

HOW TO MAKE THE ARMS

THE arms of the puppet are in two parts, the upper and the lower arm. Sometimes a puppeteer prefers to affix the upper arm to the body by means of cloth or leather strips (*Fig.* 18). I am certainly not enamoured of this method. I prefer the much more direct way of the screw-eye (*Fig.* 19).

FIG. 18

Leather strips joining arms to body at shoulder.

For the two parts of the arm you can use dowel rods or you can use—as I use—odd pieces of firewood, cut and rounded with an ordinary penknife.

The upper arm is longer than the lower.

Fasten the upper arm to the trunk by means of interlocking screw-eyes. The join makes the elbow-joint. Fasten the hand to the lower arm with interlocking screw-eyes. The join becomes the wrist-joint.

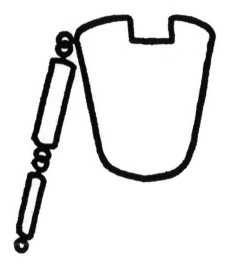

FIG. 19.

CHAPTER FIVE

HOW TO MAKE THE HANDS

ELSEWHERE throughout this work I have described several ways of creating hands for puppets.

Take a piece of flexible wire and shape the boxing-glove hand, making it taper off more suddenly than you did originally. (*Fig.* 20.)

Lay this wire shape upon a piece of chamois leather and cut out two pieces following the line and allowing an eighth of an inch margin all round the edge. (*Fig.* 21.)

Use cotton-wool for stuffing.

Use a piece of lead for weighting.

Put the lead in the palm of the wire skeleton after wrapping the lead about with the cotton-wool.

With needle and thread begin to sew the two halves of the hand-shape together, beginning at the thumb joint and working around the fingertips. Using an orange-stick, pack the cotton wool tightly into the shaping glove. Sew to the wrist and finish off. Begin again at the thumb-joint. Work around the thumb. Pack the thumb with cotton-wool. Proceed with the sewing to the wrist and finish off. Pinch into shape with your thumb and finger. (*Fig.* 22.)

Do not forget, as you bend the original shape in the wire, you pull both ends together at the wrist. Using a pair of fine pliers make a loop in one of the free strands and bury the end back into the wrist. The loop can now be attached to the screw-eye which is placed at the wrist end of the lower arm.

You may prefer to carve your puppet hands out of wood. The style will be your individual choice. Experienced puppeteers achieve lifelike effects with their delicately carved hands. You need not aim for this at this moment. My advice to you is to *symbolise* as much as possible. If your puppet hands look like hands and your puppet feet look like feet, then it is immaterial if

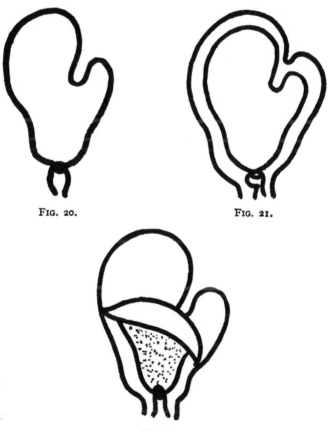

FIG. 20.   FIG. 21.

FIG. 22.

you show every crook of the finger and every joint of the foot.   More especially is this so of the foot, for in the main it will be covered, and so it does not matter a great deal what is inside the boot or the shoe. This, by the way, is no plea for slipshod work.   It is a plea for common sense in the making of the puppet.

Do not be afraid of symbolising hands and feet. Symbolise faces, too, if you feel so disposed.

And in the elimination of unessential details you begin to approach near to the standard of symbolism which is so effective upon the model stage.

CHAPTER SIX

HOW TO MAKE THE FEET AND LEGS

LET us begin with the legs first. As you required two sections to each arm, so, too, will you require two sections to each leg. There is the thigh and there is the shin.

Carve your leg parts out of scrap wood—or use dowels if you prefer. Remember that the thigh is a fairly substantial portion of human anatomy, so make the thigh a good deal thicker than the upper arm. Make the shin thicker than the lower arm. (*Fig.* 23.)

Shape the thigh from the hip to the knee. Shape the shin from the knee to the ankle. Join the thigh to the body with an interlocking screw-eye. The join between thigh and shin then makes the knee-joint. That between shin and foot makes the ankle-joint. We come now to the feet themselves.

Puppet feet must be weighty. They must function not only visibly —as feet ; but invisibly —as ballast.

You may cut your puppet feet out of wood and weight each foot by soling it with sheet lead.

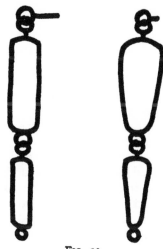

FIG. 23.

You can make your puppet feet by using a wire-shape for the sole. Then solder an upper structure of wire to represent the side view of the foot. Cover the whole in chamois leather and fill in with cotton-wool and lead shot. (*Fig.* 24.)

Or—the most satisfactory method—you may cast your puppet feet in lead.

If you are going to mould feet, arrange your moulds so that you can do several at a time and so build a store. This saves time and patience and is, anyway, the most sensible thing to do.

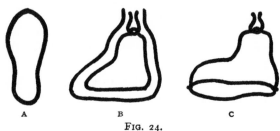

A   B   C
FIG. 24.
A—Wire foot.   B—Skeleton of foot.   C—Chamois leather covering

1. Model the foot out of plasticene. Model, shall we say, a dozen feet at the same time. Keep the models as near alike as is humanly possible. This sounds difficult, but it is not, and when you remember that children can make quite a lot of almost identical shapes in a single lesson, that alone should be incentive enough to go forward boldly with the work.

Model the feet first.

2. Now cut cardboard into strips to make a loose-sided box. For this you will want two long narrow strips for the two long sides. Two short strips for the two short sides and one large strip for the detachable base.

3. Brush pure linseed oil, or pure olive oil, or melted vaseline over the cardboard strips on those sides of the strips which will face inwards when the box is erected

There is substance in millboard which you will find a valuable ally.

4. Mix up plaster of paris and have it ready for use. Try to get someone else to help you here, for plaster of paris has a nasty habit of setting before you are ready for it.

5. You have already oiled the under surfaces of the cardboard. Now erect the box, holding the sides into position by a large and not too tight elastic band, or alternatively tie about with string. Place the four sides about the detachable base. Actually the four sides shown fit *around* the base, and not merely lodge upon the surface of the base.

6. Oil the plastic feet and place these feet well apart upon the " floor " of the box. Put them upon the " floor " in an upright position, i.e., the sole of the foot to the baseboards.

7. Pour in the plaster of paris carefully until the whole collection of feet is covered with plaster. Flood the plaster right over the ankle level.

You have the twelve feet encasep in plaster of daris with the soles untouched because they are flush upon the baseboard of the box.

8. Leave to dry. To be on the safe side leave this mould setting for two or three days so that every scrap of moisture is out of the mould.

It is a good plan to remove the cardboard after the first twenty-four hours and leave the plaster exposed to the air on all sides. This again facilitates the drying process. At this stage you can also lightly tap out the plastic feet. This will give other exposed areas for drying.

When the mould is *really dry*—and it must be dry or the lead will " fly "—you can mould the feet.

9. Melt the lumps of lead to " liquid consistency." Use a ladle for this.

10. Put a sheet of metal over a low gas jet. Upon the metal plate put the plaster of paris mould and slowly heat through. When the mould is well warmed, remove from the gas, keep it upon the plate and pour in the molten lead. Before pouring in ascertain whether the inside of each mould is oiled enough. If you think not, then brush a little oil all over the inside, using a small brush. See that no surplus oil is left anywhere. Some puppeteers like to fill the moulds with oil and then turn them upside down and drain. Then they pour in the lead.

The foot is sole upwards. You pour in the lead. It flows at once down to the ankle, fills up and runs into the instep and then flattens out at the sole.

Leave to dry.

When dry lift out.

If all has gone well, the feet will come out cleanly. If not you may have to prise the lead foot out of its plaster cast. That means a new mould. So be careful.

Some folk like to speed up the process by watching the setting lead and when it appears to be solidifying they drop the lead feet into cold water by tipping the mould over a bucket. Frankly, I would advise you to make haste slowly. There is many a slip 'twixt the mould and that all too easy bucket of cold water. What's the hurry, anyway? There is always to-morrow. . . .

11. When the feet are dry, bore a small hole into the ankle level and screw in an opened screw-eye. Now close the eye about the one fixed at the bottom of the shin. So you add the feet to the legs.

12. Finally, you will have to fix the operation point to the toe of the foot. This is the point to which the string must be attached for the manipulation of the foot. Drive into the toe of each foot a small screw-eye and that is done with.

CHAPTER SEVEN

HOW TO MAKE THE BODY OF THE PUPPET

THERE are so many ways of making the body of a puppet that one hesitates where to begin, but I think you cannot go far wrong if you make the puppet body in two parts.

There is the *torso* and there is the *pelvic girdle*. These are loose enough terms, but they will suffice.

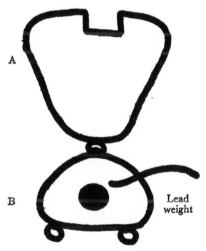

FIG. 25.

A—The torso.   B—Pelvic girdle.

The torso is carved out of wood and to the torso you fasten the arms.

The pelvic girdle is swivelled to the torso and fastened to its base are the legs of the puppet.

L

Both parts must be shaped carefully and it is advisable to weight the pelvic girdle with lead.   To add this weight bore a hole from front to back and beat into the hole some lead piping.   This will help keep the body in a vertical position when being manipulated.

Turn now to my illustration (*Fig.* 25) and follow the suggestions drawn upon that diagram.

CHAPTER EIGHT

CONTROLS

WE have seen that a puppet is a jointed figure with flexible joints. When you have made your first puppet you will discover very quickly indeed that the confounded little fellow simply refuses to stand up by himself.

Like the Saturday Night inebriate who loves his Mother Earth, he has to be held up. The puppet has to be suspended, strung up. He is held upright by means of strings.

Stringing a puppet is quite a delicate undertaking, for one must keep always in mind the problem of *balance*. When strung the puppet should hang vertically, its head in a direct line with the rest of the body.

So we have now to ascertain the exact position of the point to which the strings must be attached:

1. The strings may be fastened to the head, one string to the left of the head and one to the right of the head. The point of contact is just behind the ear on either side.

2. Next fasten two strings, one by the left shoulder-blade and one by the right shoulder-blade.

3. Now you want to operate the hands and arms, so you attach a string to the hands. One string to each hand. Bore a small hole through the back of the hand to the palm. Thread the string through and knot into the palm.

4. To operate the legs, bore a hole through each thigh, thread the string through and knot behind the thigh.

This is one method of stringing. A second proceeds as above from 1 to 3. Stage 4 is altered to :—Bore a hole through the toes of each foot. Thread the string through the toe and knot underneath. This is not a satisfactory method, for it leaves a protruding knot *under* the foot. It is wiser, therefore, to drive a tiny screw-eye into the toe or into the instep of each foot and attach the string to that screw-eye. (*Fig.* 26.)

Another method of stringing allows you to attach strings to the head points, the shoulder-blades, the hands, *the joints of the knees*, and the toe or instep.

You must experiment for yourself until you find which is the ideal method of stringing your own puppet. You may wish to make your own adaptations. Make them, but remember that the main, the only purpose of stringing a puppet is *to make it work*. It must work realistically. It must walk and move as a human being and not as Rossum's Universal Robots.

Let us suppose now that we have fastened the strings to the puppet, that the strings are correctly placed and that the puppet hangs in balance. We have forgotten two things.

First we have strung the *naked* puppet. This is excellent practice, but a naked puppet walking upon the stage will be a strange sight indeed. So string your naked puppet by all means. Get to know how to sling the puppet in balance. Then remove the strings—and dress that puppet !

The strings you must thread through the costume after the puppet has been dressed. If your points are accurately placed and if you are careful in threading the strings through the costume, then the puppet will hang beautifully. It will be " all set " for work.

So we have dressed the puppet and restrung the puppet, pulling the strings through the costume.

Now what are we to *do* with these strings? At the moment they are loose ends lying untidily upon the table.

These strings must be gathered up and linked to the *puppet control.*

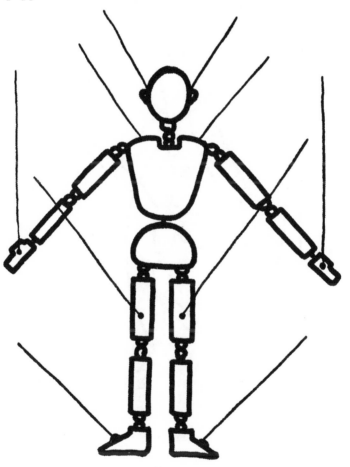

Fig. 26.

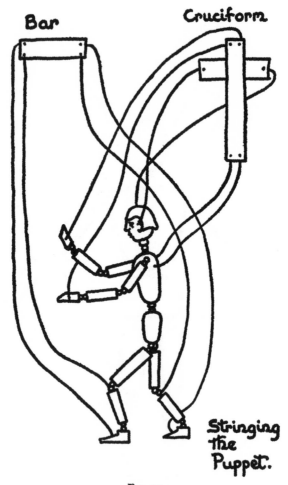

FIG. 27.

The control is made from wood and is in two parts. There is a cruciform shape and there is a bar shape.

To the cruciform shape you fasten :
 (a) the head strings ;
 (b) the balance strings attached to the shoulder-blades ;
 (c) hand strings.

To the bar shape you fasten :
 (a) the thigh or knee strings ;
 (b) the foot strings.

For this style of stringing turn to my illustration (*Fig. 27*) and follow the lines carefully.

This type suggests that you use both hands in the control of the puppet. You hold the *cruciform* in your right hand, or to be more exact you slip the *cruciform* control *upon* your right hand. There is a slip of webbing, or of felt, or of leather, through which you place your right hand until the band lies across the back of your hand, between knuckles and wrist.

The *bar* control you hold in your left hand.

Some puppeteers prefer to unite these two controls, making one of them. A glance at my illustration (*Fig. 28*) will reveal how this operates.

Your puppet is now dressed, strung, and attached to the controls. The next stage, both interesting and difficult, is to learn how to operate those controls. This I cannot advise you upon. It comes only with practice, and for the sake of your own self-respect do not attempt to give a performance until your puppet obeys every touch of the strings.

You will find that it will facilitate movement if you operate the hand and feet strings by finger-work, the fingers reaching over the edge of the controls and holding the hand and feet strings around the fingers.

Learn to make the puppet walk, bow, sit down, turn about quite naturally. Nothing looks more funny than

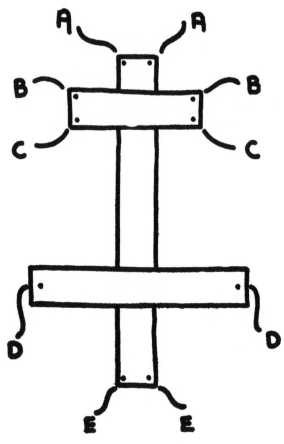

FIG. 28.

A—Hands.   C—Knee or thigh.
B—Toe.   D—Head.
        E—Shoulder-blades.

a puppet being swung about by its strings, like a child upon a wound-up swing !

Learn to make the puppet *bend* its head forward, sideways and backward ; turn to the left and turn to the right.

Set yourself a definite movement, one movement at a time, and keep on working at *that one movement* until you really are satisfied that the action is correct. Once you feel that, you can go ahead with your production, but not before.

CHAPTER NINE

STORING THE PUPPET

ONCE the strings of a puppet are entangled there is serious trouble in the camp. Unravelling a ball of twisted wool is simple by comparison.

So store your puppets safely.

To do this make little cloth bags of sufficient size that the puppet may be lowered carefully into the bag—keep the strings taut—until the whole of the puppet is *inside* the bag, and about two inches of the strings as well. Two inches of string, that is, as far as the crown of the head.

Have a draw-string at the mouth of the bag. Draw this tight and fasten. Your puppet is safely housed and if the bag does swing—the resultant cord may quite easily be " unswung."

Hang the bagged puppets from hooks at the back of the stage when not in use. Label the outside of each bag with the name of the character it contains. This saves time and temper ! (*Figs.* 30A and 30B.)

FIG. 29.

158

CHAPTER TEN

I AM assuming here that you will be building for yourself a fully equipped puppet stage. I do not want you to feel that because you have neither the room nor the facilities for a puppet stage that you cannot therefore proceed with puppetry. Of course you can, but if I give you an idea of a full puppet stage then you can see what is required and make every adaptation you feel necessary in accordance with your own particular circumstances.

The puppet stage may be in parts. There is the stage itself. This should be on the easy eye level of the audience when seated. It is perhaps advisable to make it a little *above* the eye level to allow for " the long and the short of it " in the audience.

The stage. This must be wide enough to give a good proscenium opening *plus* additional width in the wings to enable the puppeteers to move freely out of sight of the audience.

Here, if possible, curtain off the stage right across the room, so that the stage of the theatre is completely cut off from the auditorium, then no Peeping Toms can see behind and help destroy the illusion.

The wings should be kept open to allow for the free passage of the puppets, *and*—the front row of the audience should be far enough back so that it is impossible to see *into* the wings. This *is* important.

The back of the stage comprises a sturdy framework in wood. Here the backcloths will hang. But this frame will project upwards with a stout crossbar, of at

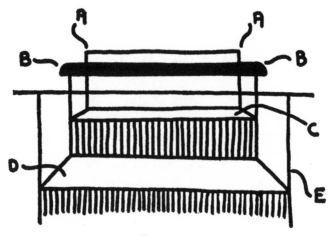

FIG. 30A.

A—Back of theatre.   C—Puppeteers' platform.
B—Puppeteers' rest.   D—Stage.
E—Frame to carry stage front and proscenium arch.

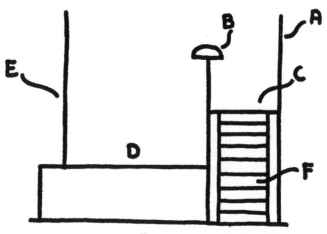

FIG. 30B.

Puppet theatre side view tabulation as for Fig. 30A.
F—Steps from floor to puppeteers' platform.

least a six-inch width, with the edges carefully rounded. This makes the arm and body rest for the operating puppeteer.

Raised above the level of the stage and at a level to allow for the puppeteers to stand and look over and operate the figures in comfort is a platform. This is the puppeteers' operating platform—a very bulwark against all unseemly happenings in this delicate world of puppetry manipulation.

Behind the operating platform is a guard rail, which serves, or can serve, a dual purpose. It can prevent the puppeteers stepping backwards too far and falling into the nether regions behind the stage, and it can serve as the storage bar for the bagged puppets. The hooks will be placed on the outside of the bar so as not to impede the puppeteers.

Steps, of course, lead up from the ground level to the operating platform.

This, then, is the basic shape of the puppet theatre. I repeat : do not be overawed by this. It will serve to show you the essentials. How you marshal or adapt those essentials you alone can decide. (*Fig.* 30.)

CHAPTER ELEVEN

PARTS OF A STAGE

NAMES are given to special parts of a stage. These names will help you, so here they are :

Proscenium.—The frame which surrounds the stage picture when the curtain goes up.

FIG. 31.

The proscenium arch, showing :—

A—Teaser.   C—Tormentors.
B—Back flat.   D—Wings.

Keep the line of the proscenium as plain as possible. No need to be affected.

Tormentors.—These are flats of scenery which run from the stage floor up towards the flies and start just behind the left and right walls of the proscenium arch.

Flies.—The region above the stage, and out of sight of the audience.

The Back Flat.—The scenery erected at the back of the stage. The backcloth.

Teaser. The curtain which hangs down and reaches across the " ceiling " of the stage.

The Wings.—These are the hidden areas, hidden, that is, from the audience, which lie left and right of the proscenium arch. (*Fig.* 31.)

CHAPTER TWELVE

THE lighting of the model theatre need not constitute a great problem. It is only when you allow your electrician friend to take complete charge of your productions that you meet with trouble.

Keep your lighting system as simple as you can. Remember that it is wiser to illuminate your stage from footlights and from vertical batten lights in the wings, than to attempt any overhead lighting. This does not rule out overhead illuminations if you want them, only keep clear of the puppet strings.

If you are like I am you will hate all forms of footlights. So place your lights behind the proscenium arch, throwing the light inwards on to the stage. Try to have each light, or each series of lights, upon a separate circuit operated by a separate switch.

Besides fixed lights you will find it advisable to have several movable lights to be arranged according to the needs of the production.

But keep to a simple arrangement. You are running a theatre, not experimenting with electricity!

CHAPTER THIRTEEN

PROPORTIONS OF THE HUMAN FIGURE

It is essential that puppets should be more or less in proportion, and here it is wise to link puppetry with the human figure. Therein lies a snag. So few human figures are in proportion, and since variety adds to the spice of life I for one am not complaining.

But we do want some sort of a standard for our puppets, so here is a suggestion for you to follow if you wish.

Imagine that the total length of the human figure is eight heads, a head measuring from the crown to the chin, then you get the following divisions:

1. Crown of head to bottom of chin.
2. Chin to a line drawn across the nipples.
3. From transversal 2 to just above the navel.
4. From transversal 3 to a line straight across the hips.
5. From transversal 4 to a line drawn across the middle of the thighs.
6. From transversal 5 to a line falling just a little below the bend of the knee.
7. From transversal 6 to a line drawn across the legs at a point a little below the calf.
8. From transversal 7 to the base of the heel.

The human face also has its proportions strange as that, may sound!

The face from the hair-line on the forehead to the point of the chin is equal to three nose lengths.

If you square-up the head, this gives you five squares in width and seven in length.

From crown of head to the hair-line on the forehead is of one square's depth.

From the hair-line on forehead to bridge of nose is two squares depth (or the length of one nose).

From bridge of nose to base of nose is two squares depth.

From base of nose to point of chin is two squares depth.

The ear is of two squares depth and the ears are in the same parallels as in the nose.

If you divide the area from the base of the nose to the point of the chin into three equal parts, the lines running across the face, then from base of nose to parting line between the lips is one part, from the parting line of the lips to the beginning of the chin is one part, and from this line to the point of the chin is one part.

You can use these proportions if you like, or you can more or less ignore them—as you like. From my own experience I think it will depend absolutely upon the type of face you intend to carve.

THE SACRED FLAME

A FANTASY IN ONE ACT

By

ARTHUR B. ALLEN

Characters :

PILGRIM	. . .	A Wandering Philosopher
SYLVIA	. . . . . .	The Girl
HALLAM	. . . . . .	The Fellow

SCENE.—*The countryside by night ; a camp fire is burning ;* PILGRIM, SYLVIA *and* HALLAM *sit talking.*

PILGRIM : There certainly is a lure of the firelight.

SYLVIA : It makes you feel comfy inside.

HALLAM : It makes me dream.

PILGRIM : And me it makes live again. I see the pageantry of fire. I see the almost perfect man worshipping his new discovered servant and his master. I see him use fire as a symbol of unity.

He uses fire for warmth, for food, for protection. It protects him from devils, from dangers in the forest. On through the ages—on and on. Fire is the centre of all human life and all human activities, until we, passing through time, reach the moment when three people, two males and one female, sit around a star-fire upon the Cotswolds. One with the joy of living in his heart. One with a heart within him which leaps up in spite of himself, but whose impulsive clutch at the nearest star is checked by knowledge of things that have been. The remaining being is atuned with Nature, for his is the way of the open air, and his mind is the mind of a child.

SYLVIA : You read so well. You know what I feel, but I've never told you. I've—I've tried to hide it !

PILGRIM : Never try to hide what you feel when you are out of doors. It's an insult to the whole universe. Register what you feel, and stand by your emotions, unshaken and unashamed. Are you ashamed of your feelings ?

SYLVIA : No. But sometimes I feel I ought not to feel as I do. I feel too happy to contain it all. We have been out here for a week, Bruce and I, up on these hills. Our tents are close together behind that copse. It's been glorious. And I felt, oh ! too small to contain all the thoughts and feelings that rush through me.

PILGRIM : You know these hills well then ?

SYLVIA : Yes. I was born not far from here. I've chased butterflies and picked flowers up here as long as I can remember. Then the city called me and I had to go—to *exist*. But I come back here to *live*.

PILGRIM : Man grows attached to the soil that first bore his weight.

SYLVIA : I used to come up here when I was worried or troubled, or in trouble. It's glorious to have the wind in your hair. Hair loves the wind. Strands of it will follow the wind even when it blows gently. A gust—and a wisp of hair says : " Let me come, too ? " It breaks away from its place and tries to curl up lovingly into the stream of air that passes, but the wind goes on and the straying strands—after several tortuous efforts to hold on—droop in despair, to be ignominiously pushed into place again.

HALLAM : That's like all of us. We are forced into our place because our spirit is either broken or ignored and we drift with the mob.

PILGRIM : You're coming on !
And so you love this part ?

SYLVIA : Yes, I do. I love it terribly. I've come up here in the rain and the sleet, with the gale so strong that you couldn't climb right to the top. The rain cuts you and stings and lashes tears to your eyes, but when you leave it, you are all aglow and your soul sings with gladness, and you face the world with spirit. There's nothing like rain-whipped skin and the mental comfort it brings.

PILGRIM : And all things fit in. The hills, the rain, the wind, your hair, your glowing skin, the pink of your cheeks and the glisten in your eye—and you.
The joy that is " you " lives because of the physical. Your skin and the rain. Your hair and the wind. Your eyes and the cold. Your spirit and—Hallam here. You all are linked together, all by Nature,

and as human beings around this fire. Everything interacts. Everything interplays. Everything is interdependent. Man must have water, earth, vegetation, air and light, before he can live. Everything makes a united whole.

SYLVIA: Go on! Go on!

PILGRIM: Above your head there bends over you a blue domed roof, studded with lights, some large, some small, all a very long way off. All singing in their respective spheres the old, old song—the song always old and ever new—the eternal song of Love. The eyes of this great blue monster twinkle with quiet humour and enjoyment. We all are a little afraid of the sky . . . if we are honest with ourselves. It's so large, so deep, and so unfathomable. The sea terrifies us with its unceasing attack and endless roar, but the sky terrifies us with its intense silence and suffocating caress.

SYLVIA: That's true. The evening light settles upon you like a mantle, and stills your voice.

HALLAM: I feel kind of choked. Something surges within you. You want to throw back your head and shout, but you cannot. Your eyes are open wide. Your throat stretches. Everything—every muscle is taut—and then you stop.

PILGRIM: Finding yourself in the presence of a mighty mystery, you cease to shout—and you worship with all your being. You are overwhelmed not by the thing itself, but by what that thing means to you in yourself. You humanise the sky. A great and unknown unknowable being suddenly rises up before you, where before was simply a blue arc with golden specks. Human nature always humanises nature.

That was the beginning of religion.

SYLVIA: I wonder.

HALLAM: I can't follow that last bit.

PILGRIM : The clouds are puffs of breath from the lips of Mother Nature. When she is pleased the puffs waft across the sky, lightly, deliciously. When she is angry her breath comes so quickly that the blue is all obscured and she speaks in thunder and lightning.

SYLVIA : You think that Mother Nature is a being then ?

PILGRIM : No. Mother Nature is everything, and everything is Mother Nature. She is the Great All that contains everything. Man tends to humanise all things. To humanise is to unite, to create one huge family. This family contains all life. Everything is life. There is no death.

Why, the very trees are human.

HALLAM : Ever seen a face in a tree ?

SYLVIA : Yes. When I've sheltered under a tree it has always welcomed me. Trees do. They are never unkind. They smile at you. They are pleased to be able to help. Their branches whisper to you when you are kind to them. They grow angry with you and shake their branches and creak and groan when you are stupid and hurt them.

PILGRIM : What do they whisper ?

SYLVIA : They whisper—I think they whisper the song you sang when you lighted the fire—*The Love Song of the Universe.*

PILGRIM : And you believe it ?

SYLVIA : I don't know yet, but when you sang it, it was as though I listened to something that I had known for a long while.

HALLAM : I felt the same, too, but one has to keep a grip on one's imagination or one gets into a devil of a fix.

PILGRIM : Never hold back your imagination. Let it go. It's healthy. You'll come out in the end. Reason is a persistent wench—she won't be buried long. Like the trees, she is always ready to whisper to you, and in an unguarded moment she'll get you.

SYLVIA: I love the idea of trees whispering and being human. They are human—so human that they speak.

PILGRIM: So does all of Nature. The thrush, the robin, the whitethroat sing away, pouring their hearts' ecstasies into the air. To be lost say you. Is anything ever lost? Nothing. Those songs go on and on, echoing—echoing—echoing. They reach the stream and the stream says: "You sing, I sing," and it babbles and gurgles with delight that it, too, may sing. It plays among the stones. They move. They roll. They "chink" together and add another note to the universal orchestra. Ths stream wraps itself round the rushes, whispering: "Come help. Come sing. Come chant. Come play," and the rushes bow, and strike up their note, playing upon each other, that another chord may be added to the refrain. The stream gurgles and trinks. The rushes play at counterpoint. The grass rustles and adds its song. The grasshopper "tzinks" and plays his part.

All those voices go out into the air and are not lost. The wind as conductor conveys all these sounds and blends them all into one melody—the unceasing anthem of the one. Softly it plays—now loudly—now a whisper—now a storm. Everything has its place—even man.

SYLVIA: How does man enter?

HALLAM: What discord does he strike? Is he the banging of the iron gate that jags one's nerves on a windy night? Or is he the scream of the screech owl? Or the cry of the infant in pain?

PILGRIM: Man enters this because he is no other than a branch. Just as the stream and the rushes are branches. (*Pause.*)

Hearken to the song of the sleeping sedges!

Hearken to the whisper of the woolly willows !
Feel the soft caress of the greater Mullein !
Watch the lithesome twining of the horny newt !
Hear the bees a-buzzing !
Catch the pollen dust—the golden dust that drifts upon its way !
List ! That's the beat of the butterfly wing setting up a rhythmic rhythm in the greater silence !
Hear the echoes of that greater silence !
There's an echo in your heart and one in yours, too !
Drink in the smells that assail you !
The overpowering scent of the heavy elder !
The timid fragrance of the peeping violet !
Draw in the strong, clean smell of the new-turned earth and the sweet sting of the fresh-cut hay.
Catch the rasp of the cornstalks as they fall groundwards and the opiate of the poppy as it falls beneath the scythe.
See the lope of the watchful hare and the glide of the fox a-slink !
See the start of the fieldmouse and the ordered shoot of the evening gnat !
See the solemn plod of the heavy-headed plough-horse ! See his complement, the heavy-footed male !
See the mind of man a-staggering—like a stilted crow !
See the lightnings from his brain ! See the genius-occasional !
See the average empty-pated idiot, breeding childer as a fly breeds flies.
Seek, oh see, the body of the not yet perfect man !
> Sing, oh, sing of the rhythmic body !
> Sing, oh, sing of the evolving mind !
> Sing, oh, sing of the imagination !
> Sing, oh, sing of the rhythmic mind !

Sing of man triumphant !
Sing of man the small.
Sing of man the mighty.
Sing the all in all !

That is what is called the vain and empty vapourings of a warped mind—which having said a lot said nothing.

SYLVIA : ROT !

HALLAM : It was great !

PILGRIM : And it means this. That man has his place with all things—and because of that he will live eternally.

HALLAM : How so ?

SYLVIA : I believe I see what you mean. (*Pause.*) You mean that since nothing is dead—man cannot die.

PILGRIM : True, O discerning damsel !

HALLAM : But I shall die.

PILGRIM : No. As a human unit you will cease to exist. You will break up and go back to the simpler forms of life from which you came. You will sleep. " Perchance to dream." You will be buried. *You* will not, but your atomic energy will live for ever in many a new way.

SYLVIA : Your breath will be in the wind and your laughter in the ripple in the cornfield. The light of your eyes will be in the starlight, and the fire in your blood in the sun. Your quietness is in the moonlight. Your joy is in the sunlight. Your dreams are in the starlight, and your energy in the bursting bud.

PILGRIM : Sing on, my dreamer !

HALLAM : Sylvia !

SYLVIA : The pliant sinews shall be in the roots of the nettles, your life in the roots of the trees. Your kindness is in the violet. Your cruelty in the sting of the bees. Your love I'll find in the silvery shower, your anger in the blustering storm. Your thoughts

in the dawn and the twilight.   Your impulse in the
babe unborn.

PILGRIM : Yes, yes.   You have the key in your hand,
the key that will open the door of revelation.   Hallam,
my son, the door lies open, won't you go through, or
are you scared ?

EVERYBODY'S
MARIONETTE BOOK

By H. W. WHANSLAW

Crown 8vo.   Cloth bound.   Illustrated throughout by
the Author.   **5/- net.**

WELLS GARDNER, DARTON & Co., Ltd.,
49 BRIGHTON ROAD, REDHILL, SURREY

EVERYBODY'S THEATRE
AND HOW TO MAKE IT

Crown 8vo.   Cloth bound.   Written and illustrated by
H. W. Whanslaw.   5/- net.

WELLS GARDNER, DARTON & Co., Ltd.,
49 BRIGHTON ROAD, REDHILL, SURREY

THE BANKSIDE STAGE BOOK

By H. W. WHANSLAW

Crown 8vo.   Cloth bound.   Illustrated throughout by the Author.

5/- net.

A Slider

Pusher

Flat Character on a Slider

using a Pusher

WELLS GARDNER, DARTON & Co., Ltd.,
49 BRIGHTON ROAD, REDHILL, SURREY

THE BANKSIDE
BOOK OF PUPPETS

By H. W. WHANSLAW

Crown 8vo.   Cloth bound.   Many illustrations by
the Author.   5/- net.

WELLS GARDNER, DARTON & Co., Ltd.,
49 BRIGHTON ROAD, REDHILL, SURREY

Ingram Content Group UK Ltd.
Milton Keynes UK
UKHW012112130723
425114UK00002B/8

9 781443 737357